33

BODY CO

T0001561

Praise for the series:

It was only a matter of time before a clever publisher realized that there is an audience for whom *Exile on Main Street* or *Electric Ladyland* are as significant and worthy of study as *The Catcher in the Rye* or *Middlemarch*. . . . The series . . . is freewheeling and eclectic, ranging from minute rock-geek analysis to idiosyncratic personal celebration—*The New York Times Book Review*

Ideal for the rock geek who thinks liner notes just aren't enough—*Rolling Stone*

One of the coolest publishing imprints on the planet—*Bookslut*

These are for the insane collectors out there who appreciate fantastic design, well-executed thinking, and things that make your house look cool. Each volume in this series takes a seminal album and breaks it down in startling minutiae. We love these. We are huge nerds—*Vice*

A brilliant series . . . each one a work of real love—*NME* (UK)

Passionate, obsessive, and smart—*Nylon*

Religious tracts for the rock 'n' roll faithful—*Boldtype*

[A] consistently excellent series—*Uncut* (UK)

We . . . aren't naive enough to think that we're your only source for reading about music (but if we had our way . . . watch out). For those of you who really like to know everything there is to know about an album, you'd do well to check out Bloomsbury's "33 1/3" series of books—*Pitchfork*

For almost 20 years, the 33-and-a-Third series of music books has focused on individual albums by acts well known (Bob Dylan, Nirvana, Abba, Radiohead), cultish (Neutral Milk Hotel, Throbbing Gristle, Wire) and many levels in-between. The range of music and their creators defines "eclectic," while the writing veers from freewheeling to acutely insightful. In essence, the books are for the music fan who (as Rolling Stone noted) "thinks liner notes just aren't enough."—*The Irish Times*

For reviews of individual titles in the series, please visit our blog at 333sound .com and our website at https://www.bloomsbury.com/academic/music-sound-studies/

Follow us on Twitter: @333books

Like us on Facebook: https://www.facebook.com/33.3books

For a complete list of books in this series, see the back of this book.

Forthcoming in the series:

Nightbirds by Craig Seymour
Ingénue by Joanna McNaney Stein
Shout at the Devil by Micco Caporale
Sandinista! by Micajah Henley
101 by Mary Valle
Here's Little Richard by Jordan Bassett
Invasion of Privacy by Ma'Chell M. Duma
White Limozeen by Steacy Easton

and many more. . .

Body Count

Ben Apatoff

BLOOMSBURY ACADEMIC
NEW YORK · LONDON · OXFORD · NEW DELHI · SYDNEY

BLOOMSBURY ACADEMIC
Bloomsbury Publishing Inc
1385 Broadway, New York, NY 10018, USA
50 Bedford Square, London, WC1B 3DP, UK
29 Earlsfort Terrace, Dublin 2, Ireland

BLOOMSBURY, BLOOMSBURY ACADEMIC and the Diana logo are trademarks of Bloomsbury Publishing Plc

First published in the United States of America 2023

Bloomsbury Publishing Inc does not have any control over, or responsibility for, any third-party websites referred to or in this book. All internet addresses given in this book were correct at the time of going to press. The author and publisher regret any inconvenience caused if addresses have changed or sites have ceased to exist, but can accept no responsibility for any such changes.

Whilst every effort has been made to locate copyright holders the publishers would be grateful to hear from any person(s) not here acknowledged.

A catalog record for this book is available from the Library of Congress.

ISBN: PB: 978-1-5013-8907-8
ePDF: 978-1-5013-8909-2
eBook: 978-1-5013-8908-5

Series: 33 ⅓

Typeset by Deanta Global Publishing Services, Chennai, India
Printed and bound in Great Britain

To find out more about our authors and books visit www.bloomsbury.com and sign up for our newsletters.

For my father, who mailed me my Body Count *CD liner notes from Virginia.*

"When the president says your name in anger, the shit has hit the fan."

—*Ice-T*

Contents

1   "Did you make 'em pay?"   1
2   "You don't wanna die there."   9
3   "Who let 'em in the club?"   27
4   "On with the Body Count."   37
5   "There goes the neighborhood."   47
6   "We're here."   55
7   "Body Count's in the house."   73
8   "Stop the car right here."   83
9   "The tension mounts."   101
10   "Just watch what you say."   113
11   "You'll be six feet underground."   127
12   "But tonight we get even."   135
13   "Body Count, motherfucker."   145

Body Count   153
Selected Bibliography   162

1
"Did you make 'em pay?"

On July 28, 1992, acclaimed rapper and actor Ice-T held a news conference at Los Angeles' Ma Maison Sofitel hotel. Ice's hardcore band Body Count's debut album, released less than four months earlier, had sold under 500,000 records but caused the music industry's biggest media storm. Other artists might've craved the notoriety, or played it up for publicity. But at the Sofitel, Ice-T put a halt to it.

Clad in all-black jeans and shirt, with alert eyes and a black No Fear baseball cap, Ice-T started the conference by screening a short film about the Civil Rights Movement and the Black Panther Party. "I don't understand why I'm supposed to like the police," he stated after the film. "They've never been a friend of Black people. As for the ones that are handling the job correctly, I have all the respect in the world for them. As for the brutal ones, I'd rather get rid of them before they get rid of me."

Ice scanned the room. "This song is about anger and the community and how people get that way. It is not a call to murder police."

"At the moment, the cops are in a criminal mode," he continued. "They've threatened to bomb the record company. I'm in the position now where I think Warner Bros. is taking the war for me. So, as of today, I'm gonna pull the song off the record."

"If you wanna kill me, come get me," Ice added. "Why haven't I received the death threats? Because they know that they can't scare me. They know that I'm not afraid of them, they know that I'm prepared to die behind this."

Ice vowed to give the record away for free at his concerts and asserted that his new record would be even harder. Asked about standing up for his free speech rights, Ice was dismissive. "The First Amendment ain't got shit to do with me. When the First Amendment was written, I was property, Black people were property," he stated. "The Constitution is a piece of shit."[1]

"The police are sending out a message to all other record companies," Ice continued. "I predict they will try to shut down rap music in the next three years."

Ice showed a video of a recent Body Count live performance. He directed reporters' attention to the outdoor crowd, a sea of headbangers throwing their hands in the air, pushing against the stage, taken in by the band's power. "Here's the problem," Ice explained. "Ain't no Black hands."

[1]Hall, Carla, and Richard Harrington. "Ice-T Drops 'Cop Killer': Rapper, Time Warner to Stop Selling Song." *The Washington Post*, July 29, 1992.

It was an issue before the dawn of rock music, from Bo Diddley remembering white appropriation in the 1950s ("It became separated, R&B became what we was doing, and rock 'n' roll became what the white kids was doing.")[2] through Body Count's spoken word "The Real Problem" in 1992. ("The problem isn't the lyrics on the records, it's the fear of the white kids liking a Black artist. But the real problem is the fear of the white girl falling in love with the Black man.") Moral panic fears of "race-mixing" that reared their head in circumstances like the White Citizens' Councils flyering the South with "Help Save the Youth of America: DON'T BUY NEGRO RECORDS" pamphlets were now visible in the Parents Music Resource Center (PMRC) sending a 1989 newsletter listing songs with warning labels, all of which were by Black artists.[3] "Chuck Berry, Little Richard and Fats Domino weren't loved by everybody in the '50s either," Ice-T said in 1990. "Now a white parent gets all paranoid when his kid says, 'I like Ice-T.'"[4]

Many of Body Count's vilifiers would have been fine with the record staying in South Central Los Angeles. But as a rock band fronted by a rapper, Body Count could be the gateway for countless white kids to discover artists like Ice-T. Ice's upcoming *Home Invasion* cover, drawn by *Body Count* cover artist Dave Halili, depicted a young white man with headphones, surrounded by violent images, plus some books

[2]*Hail! Hail! Rock 'n' Roll*. Directed by Taylor Hackford, Universal, 1987.

[3]Lusane, Clarence. "Rap, Race and Politics." *Race & Class*, vol. 35, no. 1, 1993, pp. 41–56, https://doi.org/10.1177/030639689303500105.

[4]Kot, Greg. "Rap's Bad Rap." *Chicago Tribune*, 1990, https://www.chicagotribune.com/news/ct-xpm-1990-04-15-9001310659-story.html.

(Malcolm X, Iceberg Slim, and Donald Goines) and cassettes (Ice Cube and Public Enemy), with Ice-T's looming, spectral face in the top right corner.

"The song's off the record. Shut up," said Ice. "I'm not apologizing to 'em."[5]

Of all the statements Ice-T could have made that day, this probably upset the most people. His peers, fans, and detractors all found something to complain about. CNN interviewed young fans at record stores expressing their disappointment in Ice dropping the song. Eazy-E told Howard Stern he never would have taken the song off his own album. (The previous year, Ice had called Eazy "a sucker" in *Rolling Stone* for donating to Republicans.) "The Iceman Concedeth" ran a *Newsweek* headline. "Ice-T announced at a press conference that he would no longer fight the power," reported *Billboard*.[6]

Numerous publications indicated that Ice had caved to behind-the-scenes pressure from Time Warner. "Mark July 28, 1992, on your calendars as the beginning of the end of rap music." *The Source*'s Reginald C. Dennis seethed in an editorial titled "Is Rap Dead?" "When he 'voluntarily' removed 'Cop Killer' from the Body Count album, Ice-T allowed a devastating precedent to be set, opening the door for widespread censorship of rap."[7]

---

[5]Viera, Ralph. "Ice-T / Body Count—Cop Killer Controversy." *YouTube*, April 17, 2017, https://youtu.be/AAouKLtnSFw.

[6]Griffin, Gil. "The Censorship Thing." *Billboard*, November 28, 1992.

[7]Dennis, Reginald C. "The Cops Gag Ice-T: Is Rap Dead?" *The Source*, December 1992.

"*The Source* didn't know. They didn't do any reporting on that," says hip-hop journalist Dan Charnas. "I was there, dude. That is not something that [Warner Bros. CEO] Mo [Ostin] would have done to Ice-T. But none of these people who were saying these things were there."

The day after Ice's announcement, Warner execs, artists, and managers met for an emergency summit at Warner's Burbank offices, including Charnas and his then-Def American boss Rick Rubin. Over the next several weeks, Warner and its hip-hop subsidiaries Tommy Boy and Cold Chillin' canceled upcoming releases from Paris, Kool G Rap & DJ Polo, Juvenile Committee, The Almighty RSO, and Live Squad for anti-police themes. Warner-owned Giant Records pulled out of a distribution deal with the Geto Boys. Other labels followed suit, with A&M's Intelligent Hoodlum and Hollywood Basic's Boo-Yaa T.R.I.B.E. pressured into removing police brutality-themed songs from upcoming releases and then dropped from their respective labels. Even Dr. Dre's anti-cop single with Snoop Doggy Dogg, "Deep Cover," was removed from Dre's hotly anticipated album *The Chronic*, which was blocked from release until the song "Mr. Officer" was rewritten into "The Day the Niggaz Took Over" for album inclusion.

"Mo Ostin was very contrite. He was apologetic for having to basically say, 'Hey, it's going to be a new day here at Time Warner. I can't do anything about it. They're going to be scrutinizing your lyrics. They're going to be scrutinizing your artwork. And if you feel like the scrutiny is intruding on your art, I will make it easy for you to leave, with our blessing,'" says Charnas.

Perhaps the most satisfied response to Ice's decision came from the US federal government. "I am glad that they did respond to my criticism, and the President's criticism, and the law enforcement officials' criticism," Vice President Dan Quayle stated on July 29, with House Minority Whip Newt Gingrich by his side. "They can't just hide behind the Constitution. I'm not going to get into an argument of whether this was constitutional or not constitutional, I'll just assume that it was constitutional and there was nothing illegal. It was wrong! It was fundamentally wrong."[8]

Senior publicist Bob Merlis announced that Warner would be recalling the album, and said the label had no comment on Ice's statement that the threats were coming from the police. A revised version would be in stores within four weeks. The rerelease changed the hand-drawn "Cop Killer" tattoo in the cover art to a computer typeface "Body Count." The album's last two tracks, "Out in the Parking Lot" and "Cop Killer," were replaced by a rock-fused cover of Ice's 1989 anti-censorship solo track "Freedom of Speech," featuring the Dead Kennedys' Jello Biafra and a Jimi Hendrix sample. "Smoked Pork," a skit in which Ice murders a cop, stayed on the record.

"We're not finished with them yet," said Combined Law Enforcement Associations of Texas (CLEAT) President Ron DeLord, who had spearheaded much of the campaign. "What bothered us was that this company was willing to exploit the advocation of the murder of police to earn a buck. We're not

[8]Viera, Ralph. "Ice-T / Body Count—Cop Killer Controversy." *YouTube*, April 17, 2017, https://youtu.be/AAouKLtnSFw.

going to be happy until Time Warner admits that they made a mistake."[9]

"I applaud Ice-T's decision to pull the record," DeLord told *Billboard*. "It's a first step to resolving the situation."[10]

"I kind of wanted to keep going," remembers DeLord. But a call from Phil Caruso, the longtime president of New York City's Patrolmen's Benevolent Association, helped change his mind. "He said 'Ron, it's over. We won, move on.' And I said, 'You're right.' And that was it."

On August 3, CLEAT issued a press release announcing the end of the boycott, declaring a "major victory."[11] The next day, *Body Count* was certified gold (500,000 copies sold) by the RIAA and sold out at record stores across the country.

The movement to ban "Cop Killer" had united nationwide political and law enforcement support, and without it, divisions started showing almost immediately. Several police organization leaders, the Dallas Police Association's Glenn White among them, complained that the boycott was ending too soon. "This is like Charles Manson promising to never go back to the LaBianca home again to commit a killing," stated disgraced former Reagan aide Oliver North. "We are going to pursue Time Warner to the full extent of the law in as many

---

[9]Philips, Chuck. "Ice-T Pulls 'Cop Killer' Off the Market." *Los Angeles Times*, July 29, 1992.

[10]Charnas, Dan. *The Big Payback: The History of the Business of Hip-Hop.* United States, Penguin Publishing Group, 2011.

[11]Reibman, Greg. "Boston Police Union Planning Suit against Time, Ice-T, Almighty RSO." *Billboard*, August 15, 1992.

jurisdictions as we can."[12] That summer, North had used his new foundation, the 120,000-member Freedom Alliance, to launch petitions calling on the governors of all fifty states to "apply sedition or anarchy and other criminal statutes which could be used to hold Time Warner legally accountable for its call to kill police."[13] Five years earlier, Ice-T had called out North's Iran-Contra dealings on 1987's "Squeeze the Trigger."

But while participants on all sides of the issue fumed, one activist was not giving in. "Just two days after pulling the song 'Cop Killer' from his album after a national protest, Ice-T is back in the middle of yet another controversy," *Entertainment Tonight* reported. "The singer is on the cover of *Rolling Stone*, and police are not happy about how he's dressed."[14] The show cut to clips of five different police officers, including San Diego Police Chief Bob Burgreen, plus one officer's wife, expressing various outrage and disgust at Ice-T.

He was wearing a policeman's uniform on the cover.

[12]Philips, Chuck. "Ice-T Pulls 'Cop Killer' Off the Market." *Los Angeles Times*, July 29, 1992.

[13]Morris, Chris, et al. "Bush, New LAPD Chief, NRA Assail Body Count; Cops to Sell TW Stock." *Billboard*, July 11, 1992.

[14]Viera, Ralph. "Ice-T / Body Count—Cop Killer Controversy." *YouTube*, April 17, 2017, https://youtu.be/AAouKLtnSFw.

2
"You don't wanna die there."

By the end of 1991, rap had grown into a $700-million-a-year business. That same year, the implementation of SoundScan tracking music sales showed that radio-unfriendly rap acts like N.W.A., as well as metal bands like Metallica, were more popular than previously projected, despite rap and metal consistently polling as the two most hated forms of music in the United States.[1] One of rap's biggest stars was Ice-T.

Born Tracy Lauren Marrow in Newark ("a real 'Boy Named Sue' situation. I learnt to fight real quick."),[2] Ice spent most of his boyhood in Summit, New Jersey. His mother died of a heart attack when Ice was in third grade, followed by the death of Ice's father, also from a heart attack, four years later. Ice was orphaned at age thirteen and sent to live

[1]Wise, Brian, and Annie Bergen. "Study Reveals the Music That Americans Dislike Most: WQXR Editorial." *WQXR*, https://www.wqxr.org/story/study -reveals-music-americans-dislike/.

[2]Shelley, Jim. "Ice-T: At Home in L.A." *Jim Shelley*, 1996, http://jimshelley .com/music/ice-t-1/.

with his aunt in Los Angeles. But Ice connected with the Crips at Crenshaw High School in 1974, one year after *Time* magazine had described the school as "Fort Crenshaw" for its gang violence.[3]

"My friends became more of parents to me than any parent I ever had. I got in a gang in high school because a gang says, 'I love you,'" Ice told *Creem*. "There's a lot of negative shit to it, but when someone looks at you and says, 'Yo, you ain't never gotta worry about nothing. Nobody will ever do shit to you,' that's some serious shit."[4]

Ice was an A-student at Crenshaw who joined the school's gymnastics team and singing group while avoiding drugs and alcohol. He found an identity and namesake in crime novelist Iceberg Slim, who became a wealthy multimedia star by using words (in many cases, his ghostwriter wife Betty Beck's) to depict "the life." Sharing a bedroom with his rock fanatic cousin, Ice also developed a classic rock expertise that included bands like Blue Öyster Cult and Mott the Hoople, though Ice's favorite was the darkest and heaviest group, Black Sabbath. Ice also recognized the rock in funk leaders Parliament-Funkadelic, and admired bandleader George Clinton's managerial skills in multiple projects. "George Clinton, he's just one of those people who everyone

[3]"Education: Blackboard Battlegrounds: A Question of Survival." *Time*, February 19, 1973.

[4]Petracca, Mark. "Ice-T and Andrew Dice Clay: Ice and Dice." *Creem*, March 1993, https://www.rocksbackpages.com/library/article/ice-t-and-andrew-dice-clay-ice-and-dice.

needs to do research on. He had us all talkin' a different language," Ice remembered.[5] Clinton returned the praise in a 1993 *Washington Post* interview, naming his favorite modern rock bands. "I'm so happy to see rock 'n' roll and hip-hop mix," Clinton stated. "That's why I like Prince, Pearl Jam, Body Count, and the Red Hot Chili Peppers; they're rock 'n' roll bands that are funky."[6]

"I knew enough that if I was trying to mack at some white girls, I could blow their minds with some rock trivia," said Ice.[7] But he also befriended a rock-loving underclassman who had recently moved to Los Angeles with his single father.

Ernie Cunnigan was born in Detroit and grew up an only child, spending time in local youth centers, Boy Scouts, or going to watch wrestlers like Bobo Brazil. Ernie's first influence on guitar was his neighbor Dennis Coffey of Motown's studio band the Funk Brothers and the author of the widely sampled 1971 instrumental hit "Scorpio." Coffey rehearsed with the Detroit Guitar Band in his living room, down the street from Ernie, where a curious neighborhood

[5]Stingley, Mick. "Ice-T: 6 Albums Everyone Should Own." *Esquire*, June 29, 2022, https://www.esquire.com/entertainment/music/a29037/ice-t-albums -everyone-should-own/.

[6]Himes, Geoffrey. "Classic Funk from Clinton." *The Washington Post*, December 31, 1993.

[7]Allen, Matt. "Ice-T: 'I Play One on TV, but Cops Can Still Kiss My Ass.'" *Kerrang!*, February 16, 2021, https://www.kerrang.com/ice-t-i-play-one-on -tv-but-cops-can-still-kiss-my-ass.

boy could listen in. "It seemed like there was 50 guitar players. It was probably only three," says Ernie.

"Detroit was falling apart at that time. That's when the auto industry was about to die," says Ernie. His father moved the two of them out to Los Angeles to find work, in time for Ernie to start junior high school there. "The first person I met was the leader of the Bloods," says Ernie. "'Welcome to LA, I'm the leader of the Bloods, and basically you're gonna start killing and doing drive bys.' So anyway, I picked up the guitar."

Ernie's middle school guitar teacher taught him to play right-handed, which Ernie tried for a year until he saw fellow lefty Jimi Hendrix. Ernie has since been self-taught. Ernie played on his father's porch, taking requests for "Jungle Boogie" or "Come and Get Your Love," sometimes from the leader of the Bloods, or impressing his dad with some B.B. King. "I played a lot of Isley Brothers stuff, top 40 stuff. And a friend of mine gave me a collection of cassette tapes. Deep Purple was there, a lot of Rush, UFO, all kinds of things," he remembers. Ernie listened to local AM radio R&B, like Earth, Wind and Fire, and built a homemade smoke machine to be like the Isleys. But Ernie gravitated to rock as a musician: "I ended up playing rock 'n' roll just by default—R&B did not have enough guitar pyrotechnics in it for me."[8]

In high school Ernie took the bus from South Central to West Hollywood clubs like Starwood and Gazzarri's,

---

[8]Perlmutter, Adam. "Body Count: Ernie C & Juan Garcia's Riff Lust." *Premier Guitar*, April 1, 2021, https://www.premierguitar.com/artists/body-count-ernie-c-juan-garcias-riff-lust.

checking out everyone from the Blasters and X to Quiet Riot and Van Halen. Ernie would tune a half-step lower like Eddie Van Halen ("I couldn't tell what he was doing, but I saw him play," Ernie remembers) and customize his own guitar by getting rid of tone and volume knobs. "That's really what rock 'n' roll is anyway—on and off—there's no in-between,"[9] he stated. Ernie also put in hours at the since-demolished Tiffany Theater on Sunset Boulevard. "I used to sneak in there and watch *The Song Remains the Same* so many times. I wanted to be Jimmy Page so bad."[10]

"I met Victor Wilson around the corner, who was more down to earth," says Ernie. Wilson was an R&B drummer in a band with his brother called Imported Soul. "That'd be early 1970s. He is the link between me knowing Ice. . . . They were doing shady stuff."

"Beatmaster V was a weed dealer," says Ice, using the name most people would know Victor Ray Wilson by. "Vic got kicked out of Crenshaw. I remember the security guards chased him across the quad, he threw this book in the air that had all his weed. Joints went flying everywhere . . . they kicked him out of all LA City Schools for that."

[9]Bianca. "Body Count + Bloodlust + Ice-T + Ernie C." May 29, 2017, http://conversationswithbianca.com/2017/05/29/body-count-ernie-c/.

[10]Brando. "Ernie C Talks Body Count, Duff, and One in a Million—Appetite for Distortion: EP. 56." *YouTube*, February 1, 2019, https://youtu.be/L58NKCIrAws.

"He was more of a thug, gangster, and that kind of set the tone for the way Body Count was," remembered Ernie. "He was the one to make everybody get to rehearsal because he was so hardcore."[11]

Vic also knew ninth grader Lloyd Roberts III, a bassist whom Body Count fans would know as Mooseman. "He and Vic used to sell marijuana together," says Ernie. "I met Moose through Vic."

"Moose was a lovely person," says Living Colour guitarist Vernon Reid. "He was a classic, gentle giant character type . . . this warm, very approachable person."

"Mooseman . . . fucking cool as shit dude," says Butthole Surfers' Gibby Haynes.

Ernie found camaraderie with another left-handed guitarist, Dennis Miles, who played his instrument upside down while Ernie preferred keeping the knobs up top. Body Count fans know him as D-Roc the Executioner. "D-Roc, he was the quiet one," says Crenshaw pal Sean E. Sean. "He was really under the radar."

"D-Roc was my rhythm guitar player. In high school I had a real expensive guitar. I bought a Fender Stratocaster," says Ernie, who worked shifts at Kentucky Fried Chicken to come up with the $636 for the instrument. "I can't remember bringing that guitar to school because I didn't want anyone to take it. D-Roc had a cheap guitar, and he was left-handed. I used to always take his guitar and play it in high school."

[11]*Body Count: Murder 4 Hire.* Directed by Erik Voake, Woodhaven Entertainment, 2005.

D-Roc remained the band's most private musician, seldom giving interviews. He donned a Jason mask on stage and in band photos. "That's my mentor, I follow him," D-Roc described the masked persona in offstage footage. "Actually, it came from seeing Kiss."[12]

The boys socialized in the school lunchroom, where Ice made a name for himself playing the dozens. "He was always the guy that could out-talk you. He was rapping before there was rap,"[13] Ernie remembered.

"Ernie's the most talented person I know, as far as music," says Ice. "Ever since high school, he walked around with that guitar. . . . He was playing concerts in Crenshaw High School, doing Peter Frampton and playing Led Zeppelin at lunchtime."

"I was playing the multipurpose room, and in the front row was nothing but Crips," says Ernie. "I used to make these flash pots, and I didn't know they put flash powder in there. So I put gun powder in there, I went to the gun store." Ernie poked holes in a can, connected electrical wires, and installed an on/off switch, setting off explosions while he played. "It almost caught the curtains on fire."

"Music kept us out of a lot of trouble. The gangsters liked musicians; they knew the musicians weren't gangbanging," Ernie recalled.[14]

---

[12]Ibid.

[13]Marz, Tommy. "Interview: Ernie C.: Body Count." *Sound Vapors*, April 10, 2020, https://soundvapors.com/interview-ernie-c-body-count/.

[14]Chamberlain, Rich. "Ernie C Talks Bloodlust, Producing Black Sabbath and 25 Years of Body Count." MusicRadar, March 9, 2017, https://www

As a budding guitarist, Ernie's boyhood band Ernie and the Superbads found a regular Saturday gig at the Imperial West, a club owned by Ms. Evelyn Beal, Lou Rawls' mother. Ernie also sat in for rehearsals with the legends that stopped by the Total Experience club in South Central, playing with the Temptations, Harold Melvin and the Blue Notes, the Main Ingredient, Donny Hathaway, members of War, and the Coasters, who offered Ernie an audition to play guitar. "I was too young. They wanted to go traveling, I was in high school and I really couldn't travel like that," says Ernie.

Ice graduated from Crenshaw in 1976, with a high school girlfriend and baby daughter. He enlisted in the US Army the next year, spending four years in the 25th Infantry Division in Hawaii after basic training. Like many youths, Ice loved the Sugarhill Gang's "Rapper's Delight" and got interested in hip-hop. After an honorable discharge, he hustled his way into a string of singles and local DJ stints while making most of his money as a small-time crook. Gang murders and the crack epidemic were booming when Ice returned to South Central, where government-funded housing, education, and health programs were wrecked by Reaganomics. "Jewelry-store robberies, credit card fraud, insurance fraud, burglaries and stuff," Ice recalled his criminal past. "I was riding with some bad cats."[15] Rapping and crime both came naturally to a man who was good at talk, and being sober, Ice would do

.musicradar.com/news/ernie-c-talks-bloodlust-black-sabbath-and-25-years-of-body-count.

[15]DiMartino, Dave. "At Home with Ice-T." *Entertainment Weekly*, May 31, 1991.

the talking when the cops pulled his guys over. "I knew what white people would go for," he remembered.[16]

Ice talked his way into a regular rapping and DJ gig at Los Angeles dance club the Radio, later Radiotron, where he schmoozed with new wave scenesters like Adam Ant and Madonna. At the Radio, Ice also met his future producer Afrika Islam, DJ Evil E, and cover girl/video model Darlene "the Syndicate Queen" Ortiz, who would join Ice in rap's first major power couple. "He was a natural-born hustler, a force of nature. When he put his mind on something, you best believe it was gonna get handled," remembered Ortiz.[17]

That hustle might've included ghostwriting raps for Mr. T's educational video or spitting bars about horse racing for the 1986 comedy *The Longshot*. Hollywood producers stopped by the Radio to recruit rappers and breakdancers for the *Breakin'* films, including Ice-T in a performance that might be unrecognizable to Body Count fans. Say what one will, and many have, Ice included, about the films' lack of authenticity, but they drastically expanded rap's audience. Ice brought Ernie on for *Breakin' 2: Electric Boogaloo*. "He called me up and says, 'They're filming downtown. You wanna be in a movie?'" remembers Ernie. "Those times, it was so easy. It's like, 'What are you doing today?' 'Nothing.' 'You wanna be in a movie?' 'Yeah, sure, why not?'"

[16]Tannenbaum, Rob. "Ice-T: Sold on Ice." *GQ*, March 1994, https://www.rocksbackpages.com/library/article/ice-t-sold-on-ice.

[17]Ortiz, Darlene, and Heidi Cuda. *Definition of Down: My Life with Ice T and the Birth of Hip Hop*. United States, Over the Edge Books, 2015.

"I just took advantage of every opportunity that came to me. Because I feel like I come from a background with no opportunities, so when you have opportunities, you got to take advantage of them," Ice told *BAM*.[18]

Body Count engineer Troy Staton remembers Ice bringing friends to the Bronx for his rap hustle, where he stunned hip-hop crowds at venues like the South Bronx Prospect Theater. "His crime crew was Vic, Shawn E. Shawn and Shawn E. Mac."

Ice's music took a turn with his 1986 song "6 'n the Mornin'," a catchy, poetic crime story recorded for a B-side. Writing with Iceberg Slim-levels of is-he-or-isn't-he joshing, Ice showed an early glimpse of Body Count's proclivity to make listeners laugh and gasp in the same verse. It's now one of the most revolutionary songs in rap history, often viewed as the birth of gangsta rap (Ice credits Schoolly D's "P.S.K." as the inspiration) and inspiring countless tributes, ranging from Ice Cube rewriting it into "Boyz-n-the-Hood" to Snoop's "Gin and Juice" bitches not leaving till six in the morning.

"At the time, the United States was not familiar with the LA gang scene. They'd been watching MTV, so they thought LA was David Lee Roth's 'California Girls,'" Ice recalled.[19]

[18]Mapp, Keno. "One-on-One with Ice-T and the Return of Body Count: Keeping It Real." *BAM Magazine—San Francisco Bay Area Music, Musicians, Clubs, and Events*, March 10, 2022, https://bammagazine.com/one-on-one -with-ice-t-and-the-return-of-body-count-keeping-it-real/.

[19]Lloyd, Jimmy. "Ice T Interviewed on *The Jimmy Lloyd Songwriter Showcase—Jimmylloyd.com*." *YouTube*, April 12, 2016, https://youtu.be/

Ice's talents caught the ear of Warner subsidiary Sire Records co-founder and mastermind Seymour Stein, whose signees included the Ramones, Talking Heads, Depeche Mode, and Madonna. Ice would sign on to be the first rapper on Warner, as well as Sire's first Black artist, after Stein told Ice he heard shades of Bob Dylan in his demo. "I knew who Bob Dylan was, so I took that as a compliment," Ice remembered.[20] The admiration was mutual, according to a conversation with producer Daniel Lanois in Dylan's memoir, *Chronicles: Volume One*. "Danny asked me who I'd been listening to recently, and I told him Ice-T. He was surprised, but he shouldn't have been," wrote Dylan, adding that his onetime collaborator Kurtis Blow had turned him onto rap. Dylan praised Ice-T and Public Enemy for "laying down the tracks." "They were all poets and they knew what was going on."[21]

"6 'n the Mornin'" was rerecorded for Ice's debut full-length *Rhyme Pays*, a record that opens with *The Exorcist's* "Tubular Bells" and a Black Sabbath sample, one of many Ice would use throughout his rap career, featuring live drums by Beatmaster V. It is also believed to be the first record stickered with a Parental Advisory label, not the standard black-and-white rectangle that debuted on 2 Live Crew's *Banned in the*

njQYwj8feqY.

[20]Meazemillionishow. "Ice-T Speaks the Truth Pt. II." *YouTube*, September 22, 2007, https://youtu.be/QdK9bFsp82g.

[21]Dylan, Bob. *Chronicles: Volume One*. United States, Simon & Schuster, 2004.

U.S.A. in 1990, but a tubular decal shaped like a bullet or a condom. Ice wouldn't say which. "It all depends on whether your mind is turned to sex or violence," he explained. "That tells the kids that's something in there they shouldn't hear. Naturally they can't wait to hear it."[22] *Rhyme Pays* ends with a dramatic newscaster report: "Los Angeles rapper Ice-T's records banned because of his blatant use of reality."

1988's *Power* improved on *Rhyme Pays*, propelled by the Curtis Mayfield-sampling single "I'm Your Pusher," which pioneered the rapped verses/sung hook format, while Ice stepped into Mayfield's game as a movie theme writer, finding his biggest hit to date with "Colors," the title track to a 1988 crime film starring Sean Penn. Ice also transcended coastal rivalries to be the only West Coast act on the Dope Jam Tour (Say No to Drugs), with Eric B & Rakim, Doug E. Fresh, Kool Moe Dee, Boogie Down Productions, and Biz Markie, and was later saluted by New York's own Public Enemy as "The Soldier of the Highest Degree" in the booklet for *Fear of a Black Planet.*

"I knew about Ice-T long before I got to meet him," says Public Enemy's Chuck D. "The first time I ever came to LA, the first person who greeted me and PE was Ice-T. He pulled up to the tour bus outside the LA Sports Arena in the exact same car that was on the cover of *Rhyme Pays.* . . . When he started Body Count, I thought it was a no-brainer. He knew the LA punk scene and understood the marriage between rock and rap better than anybody."

[22]Hunt, Dennis. "Faces: Rhyme Pays for Ice T." *Los Angeles Times*, August 2, 1987.

"In my book, rap is rock. If you listen to an MC, we rock the house, we rock the mic," Ice told *Decibel*. "We don't 'R&B' the mic!"[23] Ice advanced that claim with his 1989 "Lethal Weapon" video, in which a doorman tries to keep Ice off the stage: "You're not playing tonight, it's metal night." When Ice finally takes the stage, his bandmates include Ernie C, Beatmaster V, Fishbone's "Dirty Walt" Kibby and Wasted Youth's Dave Kushner.

"I would listen to metal in order to get the energy to make my rap. When I would go in and cut my albums, I'm listening to lots of punk music like Minor Threat and real fast rock like Slayer," Ice stated.[24]

"Ice knows more about metal than anybody realizes," says current Body Count bassist Vincent Price. "More than a lot of people give him credit for."

Ice took a darker, more political tone on his third album, *The Iceberg/Freedom of Speech . . . Just Watch What You Say!* The Black Sabbath and Jello Biafra-sampling opener "Shut Up, Be Happy" was heavy enough to serve as Megadeth's entrance music for years. Mooseman, Ernie, and Beatmaster V and all contribute, best of all the latter two in "The Girl Tried to Kill Me," a hilarious dominatrix story shouted by Ice over AC/DC-hearkening beats that set the bar high for rap-metal. "We were like, 'We're gonna be like Run-DMC, but we get to play more,'"

---

[23]Dawes, Laina. "Body Count's Ice-T Talks Shit but Does the Shooting." *Decibel Magazine*, June 5, 2014, https://www.decibelmagazine.com/2014/06/05/body-count-s-ice-t-talks-shit-but-does-the-shooting/.

[24]Viera, Ralph. "Body Count on Rockline." *YouTube*, April 18, 2017, https://youtu.be/BkM2x51WVSk.

says Ernie, citing "Rock Box" as an inspiration. "That laid down on the groundwork for what Body Count would become."

Ice's political and social justice sensibilities started landing him more high-profile appearances. He was the one artist recruited to speak at the Congressional Black Caucus' annual legislative weekend, appearing on their C-SPAN-broadcasted September 15, panel 1988 "Gang Violence: Impacting the Black Community."[25] Ice gave a detailed, erudite look on how American capitalism allows crime and war to flourish, engaging with cheers and applause from the suit and tie audience. "He always seemed like someone who had a certain amount of knowledge and wisdom based on his life experience," says God Forbid guitarist Doc Coyle. "Anytime you saw an interview, he always had something poignant to say."

Ice became an in-demand speaker, earning standing ovations in high schools (touring with Big Daddy Kane), prisons like San Quentin, and colleges including Yale, Stanford, Princeton, Northwestern, and Harvard, where *The Iceberg/Freedom of Speech* hit No. 1 on the campus charts. Ice also received complaints. "The feds called up and said, 'We don't think Ice-T is the appropriate person to speak to our kids,'" he recalled.[26] In other circumstances, conservatives might've lionized a gun-owning, four-year army veteran, capitalist bootstrapper embodiment of the American

[25]"Gang Violence: Impacting the Black Community." *C-Span*, September 15, 1988, https://www.c-span.org/video/?4484-1%2Fgang-violence-impacting-black-community.

[26]Light, Alan. "Rapper Ice~T Busts a Movie." *Rolling Stone*, May 16, 1991.

dream, who encouraged kids to stay away from drugs and gangs—"Go to school, gain capital, infiltrate the system and take it over," Ice told his audiences.[27] But conservatives who might've fussed about supposed political correctness stifling free speech on campuses had a different view about Ice-T, and police pulled out of security for Ice's campus talks.

Still, Ice's best-remembered speaking appearances from that era may have been on the talk show circuit. He was a frequent *Arsenio Hall* guest who was also called in to debate pundits like Rev. Calvin Butts on *Video Music Box* or Juan Williams on *CBS News Nightwatch*. Most famously, an *Oprah* appearance pitted Ice, Jello Biafra, and author Nelson George against Williams, Tipper Gore, and Rabbi Abraham Cooper in a debate about music lyrics, an increasingly contentious topic in the rap era. With the recent popularity of portable listening devices like Walkman and headphones, parents had less control over what their kids listened to, and many feared the worst. "I warn you that the lyrics are shocking and offensive to some," Oprah stated. "Believe me, your children who buy tapes and buy discs and records, who put Walkmans to their ears, know these very songs." She played a bleeped sample of an *Iceberg* song in which Ice spins a tale about the time Evil E "fucked the bitch with a flashlight" (an item any P-Funk fan can appreciate) and made the woman's breasts blink lights.

Ice's defense that the lyrics were a joke and the act was consensual did not appease the audience, which both Biafra

[27]Bryant, Jerry H. *Born in a Mighty Bad Land: The Violent Man in African American Folklore and Fiction*. United States, Indiana University Press, 2003.

and attendee Darlene Ortiz, who spoke from the crowd, say Oprah stacked with PMRC members. "I don't see the humor in proposing sticking flashlights up women any more than you'd see the humor in someone singing about stringing a Black man up by the neck," a white woman in the crowd chastised Ice, to applause. "What's the difference? I'm a minority and you're a minority."[28]

Gore raised the woman's remark in her *Washington Post* opinion piece "Hate, Rape and Rap," which conflated rape and hate crime statistics with the popularity of rap and rock music. "Cultural economics were a poor excuse for the South's continuation of slavery. Ice-T's financial success cannot excuse the vileness of his message," wrote Gore. "Hitler's antisemitism sold in Nazi Germany. That didn't make it right."[29]

But a bigger shock to the talk show crowd and participants than Ice's lyrics may have been Ice himself, brought on to be made an example of, being up for any challenge his opponents threw at him. He shoots back with the quick wit of his raps and provides knowledgeable, eloquent arguments that often leave his opponents sputtering. "I've never seen anybody take over talk shows as well as Ice-T does," says Biafra. "He's one of the smartest people I've ever met. Ever."

"I've never met anybody who could think on his feet for a quote like that," says *The Ice Opinion* coauthor Heidi

[28]"Oprah Ice-T 1990 Part 3/4." *YouTube*, February 14, 2011, https://youtu.be/Y4n9xf0HJTs.

[29]Gore, Tipper. "Hate, Rape and Rap." *The Washington Post*, January 8, 1990.

Siegmund Cuda. "I used to wonder, 'Does he stay up till 3:00, 4:00 in the morning, coming up with his one-liners?'"

Biafra and Ice later joined for a 1992 *Spin* feature, recorded in part at the Hollywood Hills home Ice and Ortiz lived in with their son "Little Ice." The couple renovated the home, over the Beverly Hills Homeowners Association's objections, with a recording studio, movie screen, and a shark aquarium behind the soundboard. "Ice's house, of course, was a very impressive place," Biafra remembers. "I said 'Wow, that's really cool. Who is your decorator?'" He matches Ice-T's drawl. "'This is all me. I've broken into enough other houses to know how to decorate.'"

But no matter how much Ice leaned into his gangster image or how much his opponents tried to paint him as a villain, he often seemed like he wanted acceptance more than he wanted to be a public enemy. He cut an AIDS awareness ad for MTV in 1988. He appeared on the West Coast Rap All-Stars charity single "We're All in the Same Gang" and in the Time Warner's ABC *Earth Day Special*, a celebrity and intellectual property showcase featuring Ice in the segment "The Planet Raps Back." In interviews, he made time to renounce his early homophobic lyrics and say he had grown. ("I didn't know nothing about gay people.")[30] He worked with truce groups like Hands Across Watts and South Central Love, and took part in Los Angeles Mayor Tom Bradley's

---

[30]"90's Throwback: The Whoopi Goldberg Show - Ice-T." *YouTube*, May 1, 2014, https://youtu.be/UImTyRHRT8M.

"Peace Weekend," with profits going to Rep. Maxine Waters' inner-city job training program, Project Build. He also brought dozens of friends off the street by giving them jobs in his home or on tour, while paying for others' funerals and supporting friends in prison.[31]

"The American Dream has worked for me, to an extent," Ice told *Musician*. "But it doesn't work for everybody. My boys still get the shakedown when they come and visit me in a four-star hotel."[32]

"Ice-T, oh my god, he always took care of all his boys. He was so loyal. And I often wonder if that had something to do with being orphaned. He found his own family," says Cuda. "He took care of everybody. And what I mean by that is, millions of dollars, took care of everybody to his own detriment."

"All I want them to do is come out and say, 'I like him.' Not get the message, not understand a word I'm saying. Just think, 'Those Black guys on the stage I used to be scared of, I like 'em,'" Ice told *Rolling Stone*. "If I can do that, that's cool."[33]

[31]Shelley, Jim. "Ice-T: At Home in L.A." *Jim Shelley*, 1996, http://jimshelley.com/music/ice-t-1/.

[32]Rowland, Mark. "Ice-T: The Code of Many Colors." *Musician*, August 1991, https://www.rocksbackpages.com/library/article/ice-t-the-code-of-many-colors.

[33]Fricke, David. "Lollapalooza." *Rolling Stone*, September 19, 1991.

3
"Who let 'em in the club?"

While Ice's career picked up, Ernie started a family and found work delivering packages in Los Angeles. A 1988 job sent him to the entertainment management company Lippman Kahane, where Ernie met a gangly, androgynous alternative rock artist in a band that was making waves.

"I saw Perry Farrell and I heard him talking," remembers Ernie. "He was trying to do this song called '[Don't Call Me] Nigger, Whitey' by Sly [and the Family] Stone, and so I was like, 'I know Sly Stone.' Sly Stone lived in my friend's house." The reclusive legend was staying at a mutual friend's home in the Pacific Palisades. "He was just passing through. Sly has always been like that, sleeping on your couch."

"Everybody was like 'What?' 'I know Sly Stone, I know how to get him,'" says Ernie. "Okay, so fast forward, I got on the phone, I called Sly, like, 'This guy Perry Farrell wants to do this song, 'Nigger, Whitey.' He goes, 'No problem, no problem.' He sounds like Miles Davis, that kind of voice."

The plan was to record the song at LA rehearsal studio Mates, for Farrell and then-girlfriend Casey Niccoli's docudrama film *Gift*. "A camera crew was there, the managers, everybody's there. So I called up Sly, and his friend says 'Sly's gone, Sly is in rehab.' So I called up to the rehab. 'Could I help?' They're like, 'Sly left.' 'Right. Oh no,'" says Ernie.

Ernie turned to Farrell. "I said, 'Uh, Sly is kind of busy now. Have you guys ever heard of Ice-T?' Perry's like, 'I love Ice-T! You know Ice-T?' I'm like, 'Yeah, I can get Ice-T over here.'"

"So I called up Ice, and said 'Boss you gotta help me out. What's going on?' He's like, 'I'm in the studio right now with Quincy Jones,'" says Ernie. "He was doing *Back on the Block* with Quincy." Ice was recording a track for Jones' star-studded, multi-platinum 1989 record, for which Jones declared Ice-T's work had "the best poetic quality of any rapper, and the strongest narrative I've ever heard."[1]

"I said, 'Have you heard of Jane's Addiction?' He said, 'Yeah, I've heard of them.' I said, 'They're doing this song, and can you come over here and be on the song?' He's like, 'Okay, when I'm finished with Quincy, I'll come over there,'" says Ernie.

Approximately one hour later, Ice arrived at Mates to record the song. "Perry says to me, 'Ernie, you got a guitar?' I'm like, 'I got one in the car.' He says, 'Go get it. You can be in this video.' So I hopped in the video. So then when it comes time for Perry to do Lollapalooza, he put Ice on, and Ice turned around and put Body Count on."

[1]Donnelly, Sally B. "The Fire Around the Ice: Ice-T." *Time*, June 22, 1992.

"We started the band, that was about 1989," says Ernie. "Ice gave me some money to do some demos." Ernie recorded five songs himself and took lead vocals for the first Body Count shows, featuring Vic on drums and Moose on bass. "We were just figuring out what the band was," Ernie recalls. Ice helped spark record label interest in the band by co-writing and performing on their song "Body Count," while Ernie sang the rest. "It wasn't my whole idea of what I wanted to do. I just wanted really to play guitar, just what I'd always done in high school," says Ernie. "Ice would come on stage, and then he started singing a couple of songs. . . . He's the perfect guy for that. So he started singing more and I just kind of said, 'You know, boss, you go ahead and do that.'"

It was never intended for me to be the lead singer," Ice remembers. "We didn't know if we could sign the group to another label while I was signed to Warner Bros."

"We were actually auditioning people to be the frontman for Body Count," says Sean E. Sean. "But all these people were showing up, it was just that look at the time, people wore make up and ruffle shirts and all that, and that wasn't really the look that we were looking for. So Ice said, 'Well, hey, what does the frontman really do? It's just a lot of yelling and screaming. I can do that.'"

"They were very discouraged trying to get into other rock bands. They couldn't find a home," Ice stated.[2]

[2]Engleheart, Murray. "Another Body Murdered!" *Kerrang!*, December 18, 1993.

Ernie has been known to give out report cards on how the band performed, himself included, after shows. "I always considered him kind of the musical director of Body Count," says Steve Stewart, a former management assistant of Ice's 1987-founded Rhyme Syndicate label and collective. "Ernie kind of ran the band, as far as getting those guys together and rehearsing and putting things on the table, because Ice had a whole other career. Three other careers."

Dave Halili brought some friends to see the band at Mancini's. "Mooseman pulled up to the gig in a convertible caddy with his huge bass cabinet speakers pushing out the back seats, Ernie thought that was mythical. The show was nuclear," he recalls. "We were all shell shocked."

"Some people in bands were critiquing us," says Sean. He recalls other musicians deriding Vic as the band's "weak link," and suggesting Body Count replace their drummer. "When Beatmaster V heard that, he just went into drill mode. He started practicing and practicing and practicing . . . he had to switch over from being a regular drummer to double bass . . . from the weakest link to the strongest link."

"He was built like a tight end," says Valley rehearsal space Bill's Place owner Mark Zonder, who remembers Vic bringing a weight set on tour with the band. "He would come in by himself, go in the room, and just blaze on the drums . . . like a workout, and come out drenched in sweat."

"I've seen them with a few different drummers. For me, it always starts with the drumming," says Guns N' Roses' Duff McKagan. "They've had really cool, imaginative drummers."

Body Count had D-Roc in the lineup by April 1, 1991, at the Coconut Teaszer. "Word got out and people saw 'Body

Count featuring Ice-T," all the ads," says promoter Chris "Hot Rod" Long. "The line was almost a quarter mile from the door, up one block and then up another block." Rockers including Megadeth's Dave Mustaine and Sonic Youth's Kim Gordon and Thurston Moore showed up to early Body Count shows, as did McKagan, who befriend Ernie and met the Body Count guys at Ice's home in the Hills. "They were all fucking wonderful dudes," McKagan says.

Body Count booked some summer shows with punk-thrashers Dirty Rotten Imbeciles (D.R.I.). "Some skinheads in the crowd started booing us," Ice recounted. "Five minutes into the set we had them slam dancing."[3]

Ernie would visit Ice with a guitar, amp, and cassette deck, and the two wrote songs to bring back to the group for rehearsal. "Quincy Jones told me, 'Some of the best producers are just good hummers,'" said Ice. "Your brain has to be able to say, 'Ok, take that up an octave,' and they've gotta be able to do it. You need really talented musicians to work with a producer like me."[4]

"We were just out there testing songs and seeing which ones moved the crowd," Ice remembers. Body Count debuted songs like "KKK Bitch," "There Goes the Neighborhood," and "Cop Killer," and jammed on a version of Jimi Hendrix's "Machine Gun," with Ernie and D-Roc trading solos while Ice updated the song's Vietnam protest for the Gulf War.

"'Cop Killer' was inspired by the song 'Psycho Killer' by Talking Heads. I was singing that song and Vic, Beatmaster V,

[3]Ice-T, et al. *Split Decision: Life Stories*. United States, Gallery Books, 2022.
[4]Received by Katherine Turman, 2021.

said 'We need a cop killer,' and he started telling me about the cops out here, what they were doing to people, and my brain just started working," says Ice. "I was like, 'What if somebody was triggered by police brutality so much they went after the cops?'"

Body Count found an opening act through guitarist Tom Morello, who had met Ernie at Madame Wong's West in Santa Monica. Morello gave Ernie a tape of his new band, Rage Against the Machine, and Ernie checked them out at their rehearsal space. "They played that first record, and then he gave it to me on cassette. I'm like 'This is badass,'" remembers Ernie. "Any opportunity I could, I wanted to put them on the show because those kids were definitely stars."

"I guess our first big break came when we met Body Count's guitarist Ernie C. He liked what we did and our 10th gig was opening for that band at the Palace in Hollywood," Morello remembered. "That was freaky!"[5]

Body Count played all over LA, with anyone from Danzig to Ministry to Warrant. "We didn't have a lane we were in," says Ernie. "It was just 'get in where you fit in.'" Body Count also stayed attuned to their contemporaries at Bill's Place, where Hole, David Lee Roth, and Stone Temple Pilots rehearsed. "White Zombie used to be in the room next to us," says Ernie. "I used to tell the guys, 'Everybody be quiet y'all, I'm trying to figure out what Rob's doing over there.' We'd listen through the wall. . . . He was writing 'More Human than Human.'"

"Man, those guys were great," Zonder remembers Body Count. "Some people didn't know what to make of it. I didn't

[5]Dome, Malcolm. "My Life Story: Tom Morello." *Metal Hammer*, November 1, 2006, https://www.loudersound.com/features/my-life-story-tom-morello.

know if they were hung up on the Black-white thing, I don't know what the hell their problem was. . . . Here are these guys, they're super nice, they're funny, and they always have a smile."

"When Ice brought Body Count into the company there was not a lot of African American heavy metal. That doesn't mean that there was none, but they had something to say that other bands didn't," stated Warner exec Howie Klein.[6] He saw the band at a club show before their demo was recorded and went back to see them again at Lollapalooza. "They were just amazing," says Klein.

"Howie was like, 'I'll sign this group here.' Then it was like, 'Ice can be in the band,' officially," says Ice.

That March, KTLA Los Angeles' broadcast of a video showing four police officers beating Black motorist Rodney King brought international attention to the Los Angeles Police Department. LAPD tactics like institutionalizing the phrase "officer-involved shooting"[7] and naming their headquarters for famously racist Watts riots-era police chief William Parker had preceded current police chief Daryl Gates. But Gates had expanded the department's use of paramilitary SWAT units while introducing methods like the PR-24 metal baton and the battering ram, a six-ton military tank with a 14-foot steel beam used to break into houses during police

[6]"Ice-T." Lovett, Mandon, director. *Origins of Hip-Hop*, season 1, episode 5, A&E, 2022.

[7]Frazier, Mya. "Stop Using 'Officer-Involved Shooting.'" *Columbia Journalism Review*, August 7, 2020, https://www.cjr.org/analysis/officer -involved-shooting.php.

raids (the "batterram" referenced in "6 'n the Mornin'"). The 1988-launched Gang Related Active Trafficker Suppression (GRATS), intended to "interrogate anyone who they suspect is a gang member basing their assumptions on their dress or their use of gang hand signals," helped earn Los Angeles America's largest urban prison population,[8] as did the LAPD's CRASH unit's (Community Resources Against Street Hoodlums) extensive Operation Hammer program, a crime crackdown based in racial profiling that arrested at least 1,453 South Central residents in one 1988 weekend raid and over 50,000 total by 1990. CRASH police were known to plant drugs and weapons on suspects, with one officer recounting, "They swallow the dope or throw it away, so we beat them up and use our own. They're illegal, they're selling dope, so what kind of respect do we owe them? That's wrong, but it's how we thought about it."[9]

If Gates' sound bites, like defending a police chokehold with, "We may be finding that in some Blacks when it is applied, the veins or arteries do not open up as fast as they do in normal people"[10] or telling a 1990 Senate hearing that

[8]Perkins, William Eric. *Droppin' Science: Critical Essays on Rap Music and Hip Hop Culture*. United Sates, Temple University Press, 1996.

[9]Westhoff, Ben. *Original Gangstas: Tupac Shakur, Dr. Dre, Eazy-E, Ice Cube, and the Birth of West Coast Rap*. United States, Hachette Books, 2017.

[10]"Coast Police Chief Accused of Racism." *The New York Times*, May 13, 1982, https://www.nytimes.com/1982/05/13/us/coast-police-chief-accused-of-racism.html.

casual drug users "ought to be taken out and shot,"[11] were not celebrated, they were also not taken literally by pundits and lawmakers who might not have given a South Central rapper's lyrics a similar benefit of the doubt. "We've been rapping about the LA cops and people like Gates for years and nobody believed us," Ice stated. "I don't like the police and I don't care who knows it. If they're beating Black people half to death for no reason, why should I love them? I've been on the other end of the stick."[12]

[11]Serrano, Richard A. and Jane Fritsch. "'Yeah, I Mean It!' Gates Says of Idea to Shoot Drug Users." *Los Angeles Times*, September 8, 1990.

[12]Hunt, Dennis. "Pop Music: Q & A: A Rapper Goes Hollywood: Can Ice-T, the Pioneer of L.A.'s Gangsta Rap, Keep His Street Edge Now That He's Moved Far from the Ghetto and into the Movies?" *Los Angeles Times*, April 21, 1991, https://www.latimes.com/archives/la-xpm-1991-04-21-ca-572 -story.html.

4
"On with the Body Count."

In May 1991, Ice released *O.G. Original Gangster*, a masterful, freewheeling, twenty-four-track epic that rocketed Ice into the mainstream and established him at the forefront of gangsta rap. The album earned rave reviews and Ice's biggest chart success to date, with "New Jack Hustler (Nino's Theme)" and the title track both breaking into the top ten on *Billboard*'s Hot Rap Songs. The record also brought the terms "OG" and "original gangster" into widespread American vernacular, one year before the G-Funk explosion. On track 18, Ice-T announced the formation of his "real Black hardcore band, Body Count." "A lot of people don't realize that, you know, rock 'n' roll is truly Black music," Ice stated, giving a thoughtful discourse on the art and directing his haters to blow him.

The song, also called "Body Count," starts with Ernie's melodic guitar intro and Ice's speech about idyllic TV sitcom life, before erupting into a full band performance. "That was supposed to be like 'Stairway to Heaven,' that minor on there," Ernie remembered the intro. "That's Ice's main lick. It's like an old Chuck Berry lick. But the way he hummed it out sounded new."[1]

"Body Count" hints at nearly everything the eventual *Body Count* record unleashed, and yet sounds like it could only be a one-off. It's a nearly six-minute punk song with a renaissance-style intro, a drum solo, and a metal breakdown. It's a metal song with spoken word, protest lyrics, loose musicianship, and a hardcore pace. Ice gives funk shout-out instructions, telling Beatmaster V to "take these motherfuckers to South Central" and Ernie C to "take these motherfuckers home." The lyrics call out the US government, police brutality, and South Central gang warfare, while addressing listeners who think reality is *The Cosby Show*. Thrash metal, hardcore punk, and gangsta rap were all thriving in LA counterculture, but no one had tried them all on one record yet, much less one song.

"I must have rewound that song 'Body Count' a thousand times," remembered Canadian hard rocker Danko Jones. "I saw people who were other people of color doing a music that I loved but was dominated by white people. And I felt like a part of a group."[2]

---

[1] Angle, Brad. "Firestorm: Body Count's Ice-T and Ernie C Look Back on the Making of – and Reaction to – Their Polarizing Self-Titled 1992 Debut Album." *Guitar World*, June 2022.

[2] Jones, Danko. "Episode #188: Ernie C (Body Count)." *The Official Danko Jones Podcast*, Audioboom, 8 Feb. 2019, https://audioboom.com/channels /4937742-the-official-danko-jones-podcast.

"They've brainwashed people into believing that rock is guitars and R&B is not," Ice stated in *Q*. "Whereas you listen to Isley Brothers or Prince, and it's all rock 'n' roll."[3]

"We were just high school friends playing on a song," Ernie told MusicRadar. "There was no master plan, it just happened. It was just a way for us to stop borrowing money from Ice."[4]

"This is ghetto metal, who else is doing it?," says Staton. "Body Count's some original shit, there was no mold to follow."

"We were trying to come up with a name that meant 'Black kids.' And on Sunday, the news in LA comes on and they say, 'Fifteen youths killed this weekend in gang homicides. Now sports.' It's like a body count that comes on every weekend," Ice explained the band name on *Rockline*. "And I said, 'Wow, I guess that's what I am.' I'm just a number, I mean, it's not like we're going to investigate any of these murders or anything."

"Also, it meant how many bands we had to annihilate before we got our full respect," Ice added. "It also means how many kids get wasted in the pit. . . . It also means how many nonbelievers we can turn into believers. We call those statistics. And then has another little underground meaning

[3]Gill, Andy. "Ice-T." *Q*, September 1991, https://www.rocksbackpages.com/library/article/ice-t.

[4]Chamberlain, Rich. "Ernie C Talks Bloodlust, Producing Black Sabbath and 25 Years of Body Count." MusicRadar, March 9, 2017, https://www.musicradar.com/news/ernie-c-talks-bloodlust-black-sabbath-and-25-years-of-body-count.

about how many girls they get backstage. But we'll move on from that one. It means a lot of things, but it's a body count."[5]

"I thought that was like the most over the top name for a band," says Fishbone's Angelo Moore. "It must be on a genocidal tip, right?"

"[Perry Farrell] said, 'Hey, I'm thinking about putting together this traveling thing. You know, I want a rapper.' I said, 'Yeah, well, I'd love to do it,'" says Ice. "But then they told me I had an hour . . . I said, 'Well, I'll split my set. I'll do half rap, half rock.' And we just nailed everybody to the fucking wall."

For the first-ever Lollapalooza tour in 1991, Ice was invited to share a stage with Siouxsie and the Banshees, Living Colour, Nine Inch Nails, Butthole Surfers, Rollins Band, Violent Femmes, and Fishbone, in a celebration of alternative music and culture that also served as headliners Jane's Addiction's farewell tour. As the only rap act on the bill, Ice was the first rapper many people were seeing. "I think Ice saw that he had to cross over to an audience who had probably heard of him and maybe heard some of his music, but that he really had to reach them to make an impact. I think he worked on that as the shows went on. He would talk about different neighborhoods and tell stories from his life," says Henry Rollins.

In recordings of Ice's set, he charms and humors the fans with his banter, almost effortlessly getting crowds to sing along with songs they're learning on the spot. He makes cracks about punching bags like Daryl Gates and contemporary pop

[5]Viera, Ralph. "Body Count on *Rockline*." *YouTube*, April 18, 2017, https://youtu.be/BkM2x51WVSk.

stars while shouting out metal favorites like Slayer, Anthrax, and Megadeth. About thirty minutes through his set, he tells the crowd he's going to show them something.

"At the end of my set, I said, 'Now I'm about to prove to you that rock 'n' roll has nothing to do with color. It's a state of mind,'" says Ice. "The guitars cranked up and bam, we just came and hit it and the mosh pits went crazy."

Body Count weren't even mentioned on most Lollapalooza posters. A *Melody Maker* review captured the moment. "The beat is only punctuated by the sound of jaws dropping. Both audience and the bands watching at the side of the stage just stare in amazement and the mosh pit starts to burst when Ice yells, 'This ain't no fucking Bob Hope show, get off your fucking asses.'"[6]

"It was the first something like that happened," remembers Staton. "They'd walk out, drop the curtain, drums were there, guitar players, bass player were there, and then they'd just go right into the rock set."

"It was really good for Body Count as a new band because we only knew like seven songs, six songs," says Ernie. "Everyone was waiting for our record to come out to see what else we could do."

On stage, Sean E. Sean and Sean E. Mac joined the band as gun-toting hypemen. "We were like props for Body Count," says Sean E. Sean. "We had Pendletons on with Locs sunglasses, and our job was just to really pose behind the band."

"They were just incredible. They were really South Central dudes, really into the music, really into metal. You could talk

[6]Westenberg, Kevin. "Lollapalooza." *Melody Maker*, August 17, 1991.

to them forever about Slayer, all that stuff," says Living Colour's Corey Glover. "Every night, they were just mangling people."

"Their set didn't seem canned or put on, they were into it, and it came across completely," says Rollins. "I thought they went for it hard all the times I saw them."

"White people don't come to my shows 'cause they think they'd get their ass kicked," Ice told *Melody Maker*. "I'm glad I can come out here and show them there's nothing to be afraid of. Also, my ability to transform rap into hardcore lets people know there's not much difference."[7]

"Ice-T drove the bus for [Body Count's] crew. If he didn't drive it the entire time, then he pulled into the venues and exited the venues while driving it, just to make it look like he was driving their bus the entire time, but I suspect, that Ice-T, drove their bus the entire time," says Gibby Haynes.

"I remember 'Cop Killer' stood out because there was a lot of violence going on in the streets," says Moore. "So of course, that's why Body Count would come up that song. . . . Because the cops are killing people."

Ice and Ernie occasionally joined Jane's Addiction for "Don't Call Me Nigger, Whitey." Ice and Farrell took turns yelling the epithets at each other and raising their arms in salute (Ice's Black Power vs. Farrell's *Sieg Heil*) before embracing in a dance Farrell called "a ho-down or, like, this skank tango,"[8] while the musicians powered through the

---

[7]Ibid.

[8]Staff, *Rolling Stone*. "Perry Farrell's Favorite Lollapalooza Memories." *Rolling Stone*, June 25, 2018, https://www.rollingstone.com/music/music -news/perry-farrells-favorite-lollapalooza-memories-86547/.

song. "That's a serious song," Ice stated. "But Perry's edgy, you know? He knows how to push buttons. So I trusted him and followed his lead because he's anti-racism, he's anti-all that stuff. He's all about positive shit."[9]

Rollins joined Body Count for "There Goes the Neighborhood," a Sabbathian new song confronting white supremacy. "'There Goes the Neighborhood' is such a sadly ringing truth from coast to coast," says Rollins. "Ta-Nehisi Coates lays out the struggles Black families have had trying to own a home in his book *We Were Eight Years in Power: An American Tragedy* that 'There Goes' explains from the terrified white person's perspective. It's a smart lyric."

"I had lunch with Ice almost every day on the Lollapalooza tour," Rollins adds. "He's completely brilliant. Also, very funny." Rollins would also join Body Count for a fierce, barefoot performance at the Palace in Los Angeles, which included a stage-diving Duff McKagan.

"I appreciate the fact that they didn't have just one African-American rock 'n' roll band," says Vernon Reid. Living Colour's marvelous newest album *Time's Up* had won them a Grammy and the cover of *Rolling Stone*. Fishbone were riding on their greatest chart success with the powerful single "Sunless Saturday," which got an *SNL* performance and a music video directed by Spike Lee. But Body Count distinguished themselves by being less colorful, musically

---

[9]Bienstock, Richard. "Lollapalooza, 30 Years Later: Founder Perry Farrell Looks Back on 'Shooting for Eternity'—and What's Next." *Variety*, July 29, 2021, https://variety.com/2021/music/news/lollapalooza-30-years-perry-farrell-ice-t-1235029830/.

and visually, than the other bands, showing none of Living Colour's neon flair or Fishbone's flashy dress. Body Count's members dressed in black, often in gear that represented Rhyme Syndicate.

Attendees inevitably pitted the bands against each other, but perhaps most of all Living Colour and Body Count. A 1991 *Rolling Stone* profile by David Fricke showed Ice-T and Living Colour drummer Will Calhoun praising each other's bands. "The most striking juxtaposition of sound and vision on the bill is that of Ice-T and Living Colour," wrote Fricke. "Ice hits the stage with his posse, firing a pistol in the air and shouting, 'Fuck the police'; Living Colour rams its message of cultural celebration and racial responsibility home with avant-metal ferocity."

"Living Colour is Black. We are niggers," Ice laughed in the profile.[10]

"The fact that we're an East Coast band and they're very much a West Coast band was an interesting symmetry. Especially at that time, because the East Coast-West Coast rivalries in hip-hop were very present," says Reid. Living Colour was born in part from the Black Rock Coalition, an all-Black artists' collective and nonprofit whose cofounders included Reid and author Greg Tate. But if the BRC supported and promoted misfit artists, Body Count were misfits among the misfits. "We were in this weird middle area, between the mainstream and the alternative, we were

---

[10]Fricke, David. "Lollapalooza." *Rolling Stone*, September 19, 1991.

outsiders," stated Reid. "And Body Count, in their own way, were really outsiders."[11]

Body Count were often marginalized in discussions of great Black rock bands. Maureen Mahon's extensive book *Right to Rock: The Black Rock Coalition and the Cultural Politics of Race* does not mention Body Count. The Kandia Crazy Horse-edited *Rip It Up: The Black Experience in Rock 'N' Roll* includes interviews with Little Richard, Slash, and Lenny Kravitz, among others, but doesn't note Body Count until the book's glossary. The 1990s episode of an NPR feature titled "The Black Innovators of Rock and Roll" only delved into Living Colour and Fishbone.

"When I first started, I wanted to be in the Black Rock Coalition," says Ernie. "And they didn't feel me, you know what I mean? But I told Vernon about it, and this and that, and he was really cool."

"It was almost like the changing of the guard. It was kind of like, getting away from getting dressed up," says Ernie. "We came out as we were, we were coming out straight from the street. Nirvana kind of set it up for us to happen."

For a rap fan, it might have been the opposite. "You had Black kids into hip-hop, watching MTV for alternative videos, getting into the Red Hot Chili Peppers," stated Talib Kweli in a *Spin* article about Nirvana's hip-hop fan base. "Then Ice-T came out with Body Count. I think all that set the stage for Nirvana."[12]

[11]Fricke, David. "Live in the '90s." *Rolling Stone*, September 30, 1999.

[12]Soderberg, Brandon. "Hood Pass 4 Life." *Spin*, August 2011.

"Whenever Body Count's set was going to go down, I remember the police presence was changed," says Reid. "There was a kind of vibration that would happen with the police coming through . . . it wasn't every show, but I was like, 'Wow, where all these cops coming from?'"

Rollins confirmed this in an anecdote about the tour's Dallas stop. "I'll never forget that. Lines of cops just walking through the backstage complex, just these little militia lines seeing anybody they could find from the Body Count crew, and just vibing them. Mooseman, bass player, big dude, knocks on our door and asks [whispers] 'Can I come in and stay in here?'"[13]

Melody Maker reported police backstage in Phoenix "glowering at anyone from the Rhyme Syndicate and ominously patting their holsters," unamused by Body Count's "187 ALL COPS" T-shirts. "It's payback time," says Ice, eying an officer. "They better come correct if they come at me."[14]

Lollapalooza wrapped up in August, having brought some of music's greatest iconoclasts to packed amphitheaters across the United States and setting the stage for the alternative 1990s. "We met Butthole Surfers, got to hang out with them, became like best friends with Henry Rollins, Living Colour was out there . . . it's kind of like you're on a tour, but every night you get to go to a Jane's Addiction concert," says Ice. "There's always a great show at the end of the night."

"That was the best tour I've ever been on."

[13]Rollins, Henry, et al. "No Sell Out." *Axcess*, May 1995, http://www.comeinandburn.com/archive/soldout.htm.

[14]Westenberg, Kevin. "Lollapalooza." *Melody Maker*, August 17, 1991.

5
"There goes the neighborhood."

While rap was still new enough for many to think it was a fad, it was clearly popular enough to cash in on. Low-budget American films like *House Party* and *Boyz N the Hood* reaped box office profits. Director Mario Van Peebles offered Ice a part in Warner Bros. film *New Jack City*, a crime thriller which increased the stature of its stars Wesley Snipes, Ice-T, and Chris Rock, creating an influence that lives in everything from the rap label Cash Money Records to popularizing the boycott term "canceled," as in "cancel culture." Ice overcame his concerns about being cast as a police officer, even one who's boss enough to match wits with Wesley Snipes and record the best song for the film's hit soundtrack. "I played the cop I wish all cops were like,"[1] he told NPR's Terry Gross while assuring the *LA Times*, "Just because I play a cop doesn't

[1]"Rapper and Actor Ice-T." *Fresh Air* Archive: Interviews with Terry Gross, May 16, 1994, https://freshairarchive.org/segments/rapper-and-actor-ice-t-0.

mean I am a cop or that I like cops."[2] But by playing a cop, Ice set himself up for a longer acting career than he would have by playing a rapper. In a 1991 *Entertainment Weekly* story, Ice expressed admiration for Cher. "She'd do *Silkwood*," he explained, "then flip and be butt naked on a battleship, and nobody would question it. Because that's her singing, not her acting."[3]

"The feeling in the 'hood is, if you leave you're selling out. I would like to know who invented that idea," Ice told *Musician*. "I don't think it was nobody Black."[4]

That summer, *O.G. Original Gangster* became Ice's fourth consecutive gold record. *Rolling Stone* gave a shared lead review to *O.G. Original Gangster* and the *New Jack City* soundtrack, both earning four-star raves. He was a go-to rapper for Hollywood, dropping the only rap song on the predominately retro-sounding *Dick Tracy* soundtrack and appearing on a conspicuous poster in the *Home Alone* house. Interviewers wrote fawningly of him. It was easy to love this witty, charismatic, streetwise guy, whose drive and intellect made people feel like he was elevating them.

[2]Hunt, Dennis. "Pop Music: Q & A: A Rapper Goes Hollywood: Can Ice-T, the Pioneer of L.A.'s Gangsta Rap, Keep His Street Edge Now That He's Moved Far from the Ghetto and into the Movies?" *Los Angeles Times*, April 21, 1991.

[3]DiMartino, Dave. "At Home with Ice-T." *Entertainment Weekly*, May 31, 1991.

[4]Rowland, Mark. "Ice-T: The Code of Many Colors." *Musician*, August 1991, https://www.rocksbackpages.com/library/article/ice-t-the-code-of-many -colors.

Ice was also an unlikely star at Time Warner, which had merged Warner Communications and Time, Inc. into an unprecedented $18 billion media conglomerate in 1989. "There was a lot of good feeling towards Ice-T," says Merlis. "He was a fixture in that building. He liked to come into the building and talk to the executives and plan things."

"Ice-T blew away every stereotype that the underexposed Warner staff might have held," Charnas recounted. "He could hold forth in any conversation, whether it was about politics, sports or rock 'n' roll. He remembered your name. He recorded cool outgoing messages for your voice mailbox."[5]

Jorge Hinojosa, Ice's workaholic manager since 1983, negotiated a three-part DC Comics series called *Ice-T's Players* ("Buy it before it's banned")[6] with DC president Jenette Kahn and four pilots of an HBO series called *Ice-TV* (a blaxploitation-themed show that wrapped production with appearances from Brother Marquis, Little Richard, Quincy Jones, Queen Latifah, Flavor Flav, Isaac Hayes, Ron O'Neal, and a man *Billboard* was still referring to as "Will 'Fresh Prince' Smith.")[7] Plans were made for a possible *Players* screen adaptation, as Ice was now an in-demand Hollywood actor, picking up roles alongside Denzel Washington and John Lithgow in *Ricochet* and Ice Cube and Bill Paxton in

---

[5]Charnas, Dan. *The Big Payback: The History of the Business of Hip-Hop*. United States, Penguin Publishing Group, 2011.

[6]Zeck, Mike. "Misc. DC." *Mike Zeck Checklist*, https://mzchecklist .myportfolio.com/misc-dc.

[7]Morris, Chris. "HBO Scraps Plans to Run Program Featuring Ice-T." *Billboard*, March 6, 1993.

Looters. A clothing line, OGG: Original Gangsta Gear, was in the works for 1993.

Hinojosa and Ice also pitched an approximately $10-million "synergy" deal to Time Warner president Gerald Levin, somewhat like the nearly $60-million one Ice's labelmate Madonna had negotiated for her entertainment company, Maverick. Levin seemed receptive. "Society pokes ghetto kids down, tells them there's nothing they can do," Ice stated. "I'm trying to show that we can make our own records, run our own record companies, start our own clothing lines, make our own movies."[8]

Ice's next move, however, was Body Count's debut album. "We were going to get some big time producers to do it, and they were charging so much that we're just like, 'We'll do it ourselves,'" says Ernie. The group recorded at One on One in North Hollywood, hoping for the kind of production Bob Rock achieved there with Metallica's Black Album. Ernie produced the record himself and hired Rock's second engineer, Ulrich Wild. "He knew all the tricks Bob Rock did," said Ernie.[9]

"Ernie is a great guy, and he is probably giving way too much credit," says Wild.

---

[8]"A Year after Cop Killer, Rapper Ice-T and Body Count Back on Road as Role Models." *The Ottawa Citizen*, December 30, 1993.

[9]Angle, Brad. "Firestorm: Body Count's Ice-T and Ernie C Look Back on the Making of – and Reaction to – Their Polarizing Self-Titled 1992 Debut Album." *Guitar World*, June 2022.

"We were winging it," says Ernie. "We didn't know how to do a rock record. But Body Count was a band from the street . . . if we were to get some big producer to make us sound too slick, we wouldn't get the same impact."

At One on One, Body Count recorded guitars live and competed with the noise of the Los Angeles Metro being installed underground. ("We had to stop recording for hours at a time," says Ernie.) "We had an awful lot of fun doing it," remembers engineer Bernard Matthews, who describes a professional atmosphere ("not a lot of takes, not a lot of punches") but compares Body Count's behind-the-scenes humor to a Mel Brooks setting. "The songs were pretty well developed before we got to the studio," he adds. "When Ice-T showed up that's sort of when the party started . . . he showed up with a full entourage."

"Mooseman was a really easygoing cat," says Matthews. "Beatmaster, he did a great job. More business-like. . . . We placed the cabinets on either side of the kick drum, so every time he hit his kick drum, it was just this crushing boom in the room."

"Ernie C was definitely the driving force. . . . Certainly the dominant guitar player."

Body Count recorded the album through December and booked a busy touring schedule ("81 shows in 84 days"), gearing up for their biggest year yet.[10] "I write all of my

[10]Viera, Ralph. "Body Count on *Rockline*." *YouTube*, April 18, 2017, https://youtu.be/BkM2x51WVSk.

music for the stage," Ice told *Decibel*.[11] One hears such in the immediate, call-and-response hooks of *Body Count* songs, most of which feature the bandmates shouting back to Ice-T during the chorus, perfect for audience participation. "Once you hear our songs, the second time you hear it, you should be able to sing along with it," stated Ice.[12]

Of Ice's innumerable talents, the stage might be his very best. He manages stage divers and organizes mosh pits like a hardcore pro. Ice himself stage dives and crowd surfs in 1990s Body Count footage, catching fans' hands while they carry him back to the stage. His sharp banter has the fans hanging on every word. He strips shirtless and is sometimes down to his boxers by the show's end, acting out the most graphic parts of "Voodoo" and "Evil Dick." He headbangs and air guitars as convincingly as any metalhead. "You want to make this music, you got to go into the audience, see what they're feeling. It helps you make it," Ice told *The Wire*.[13]

"When you would watch James Brown you were in James Brown's fucking world the whole time. Slayer took you to hell and you were in it until they ended the last note," Ice stated. "With us I wanted to have multiple zones that were just as

---

[11]Dawes, Laina. "Body Count's Ice-T Talks Shit but Does the Shooting." *Decibel Magazine*, June 5, 2014, https://www.decibelmagazine.com/2014/06/05/body-count-s-ice-t-talks-shit-but-does-the-shooting/.

[12]Received by Katherine Turman, 2021.

[13]Barnes, Mike. "Invisible Jukebox: Ice-T." *The Wire*, July 1996, https://www.rocksbackpages.com/library/article/invisible-jukebox-ice-t.

good. So you got the fun zone, the punk zone, the political zone, the gangster zone."[14]

"I don't think any recording of Body Count has ever come close to some of the shit they hit on stage," says engineer Bobby Brooks. "They were all hustlers . . . Mooseman and D-Roc had T-shirts and hat-making machines that they took on the road with them. So they were doing their own merch in the hotel rooms, and maybe on the fucking bus."

"They're so unique. And he says the most hilarious stuff between songs," says 1992 Body Count tourmate Max Cavalera of Sepultura. "It's never scripted."

"The audiences were fully integrated groups of people," Matthews remembers early Body Count shows. "Hardcore hip-hoppers and hardcore metalheads getting along and just digging the show. Not since London in the '60s when the skinheads and the reggae guys were getting together have I seen that . . . that record sort of normalized that kind of an integration of audience."

"We were told that there would be crowds that would be body-slamming, and that they would come on stage and stab me." D.K. Dyson of Black Rock Coalition band Eye & I remembered opening for Body Count. "When we start, the

[14]Baltin, Steve. "Q&A: Ice-T on Always Being Real, James Brown, Ozzy Osbourne, Body Count's Grammy Nomination and More." *Forbes*, December 28, 2020, https://www.forbes.com/sites/stevebaltin/2021/12/28/qa-ice-t-on-always-being-real-james-brown-ozzy-osbourne-the-grammys-and-more/?sh=22a4bf5f5541.

crowd starts bobbing up and down—they are really the most loving, hard-looking folks I've ever seen."[15]

"Music is the most unifying thing in the world," Ice stated. "I've always been able to look at my audience and see every color, every race, every sex, everybody enjoying themselves."[16]

---

[15]Locey, Bill. "Eye & I: First Person Ocular: The Brooklyn band opening Ice-T's show is like Mister Rogers appearing with Andrew Dice Clay." *Los Angeles Times*, March 26, 1992.

[16]Angle, Brad. "Firestorm: Body Count's Ice-T and Ernie C Look Back on the Making of – and Reaction to – Their Polarizing Self-Titled 1992 Debut Album." *Guitar World*, June 2022.

6
"We're here."

It starts with the rain. Any metal record starting with rain is going to channel the birth of metal itself—Black Sabbath's "Black Sabbath," the first song on their first album in 1970, twenty-two years before Body Count's self-titled first song appeared on their self-titled debut. Like Sabbath, Body Count's album cover featured a lone, sinister figure with a similar dusked color combination. It's audacious, but *Body Count* lives up to its ambitions, not by mimicking Black Sabbath but by reinventing rock music.

Record handlers found themselves staring down a point-blank revolver aimed by a Black hand on the album's back cover. Ernie recalled a gun-flaunting album ad getting rejected from Sunset Boulevard. "Anybody else can have guns, but Black kids from South Central LA who are mad at the cops . . . not a good idea," said Ernie.[1] The first track is "Smoked Pork," a funny and fatal exchange with a policeman, also voiced by Ice, that plays out like a macabre after-hours radio drama.

Biafra grins while reciting "Smoked Pork" from memory. "How did they get away with this on a major label?"

Rap interludes were still a relatively new innovation in 1992, before skits would overrun albums, and were almost nonexistent on rock records. But Body Count adapts for the CD era by keeping nearly all the interludes to just a few seconds and by making the tracks separate from the songs. "Smoked Pork," "Now Sports," "A Statistic," "The Real Problem," "Oprah," and "Out in the Parking Lot" are short, funny, or poignant enough to be playable while concise enough to not slow down the record's pacing or distract from the songs. "Now Sports" skewers the media's indifference to gang violence, and "A Statistic" ("At this moment there are more Black males in prison than in college") arrived ten years before the Justice Policy Institute's 2002 report "Cell Blocks Versus Classroom" broadened the idea in America's consciousness. While more complete data complicates the report's findings, "A Statistic" was the first time many listeners heard and considered that message. We certainly weren't getting it from school or the news.

Body Count has eighteen tracks, twelve without counting spoken interludes, which gives it both the sprawl of hardcore

---

[1]Angle, Brad. "Firestorm: Body Count's Ice-T and Ernie C Look Back on the Making of – and Reaction to – Their Polarizing Self-Titled 1992 Debut Album." *Guitar World*, June 2022.

punk classics and the more succinct feel of the era's thrash metal. "Smoked Pork" goes right into "Body Count's in the House," the police sirens playing under the riffs and chants. "It was such a shock in terms of that sound," says *What are You Doing Here? A Black Woman's Life and Liberation in Heavy Metal* author Laina Dawes. "Even though I would say they're a straight metal band, there's also a sense of groove . . . that Black sound mixed with the heavy guitars and the rhythm section, it was this really nice blend that still had that beat, hip-hop beats where you could still move your head to it."

When Body Count's in the house, it's both a party and a home invasion, depending on the listener. Early on the record, Body Count use 1990s MC tropes like band shout-outs, "make some noise," shouting the year, and announcing that they're in the house over palm-muted metal riffs and guitar solos. In "Momma's Gotta Die Tonight," Ice shouts out the places he's taking the burnt, carved-up pieces of his mother's corpse to, the way another MC might name drop cities or towns. "I grew up in the days of Black Sabbath and Dio," Ice stated. "They're just trying to scare the shit out of people, right? So we asked the question: what's more scary than a fucking gun in your face? The Devil? Fuck that— how about a .357 [Magnum]? And that's why in the Body Count album, when you open it up, all of sudden someone's pointing a gun at ya."[2]

[2]Rowley, Scott. "The Record That Stopped the World: The Outrage and the Comedy behind Body Count's Cop Killer." *Metal Hammer*, June 1, 2020, https://www.loudersound.com/features/body-count-story-behind-cop-killer.

"We wanted to relay the Black experience, the inner city experience," said Ernie. "We wanted to put that energy forward so everyone could understand what we go through."[3]

"They were real cats. A lot of times, people would look at them and wonder if they were real musicians or real bangers, and they were both," says Chuck D. "To me, that's the world's scariest band. Their presence was, 'We ain't gonna bite off bats' heads or come with any Satanic shit. We're going to come with shit that will really scare y'all.'"

But Satan is also a tradition in Black music, long before the Devil's tritone kicked off *Black Sabbath*. "To emphasize Black Sabbath's contribution of occult concerns to rock is to forget Robert Johnson's struggles with the Devil and Howlin' Wolf's mediations on the problem of evil," wrote Robert Walser in *Running with the Devil: Power, Gender, and Madness in Heavy Metal Music*. "The debt of heavy metal to African-American music making has vanished from most accounts of the genre, just as Black History has been suppressed in every other field."[4] In the furious "Bowels of the Devil," Body Count applies Satanic metal imagery to the song's incarceration themes, lost souls and homeboys alike fed through the steel and concrete demon, released in a raging punk monster that Ernie named as his *Body Count* favorite in *Guitar World*.

[3]"Body Count: Finally We're Recognized for Good Songs, Not Just Color." *YouTube*, August 4, 2017, https://youtu.be/luWIAiYmQCY.

[4]Walser, Robert. *Running with the Devil: Power, Gender, and Madness in Heavy Metal Music*. United States, Wesleyan University Press, 2014.

"'Bowels of the Devil' is the dopest jam on there, perfect proto-thrash style punk," says Halili. "The debut album is incredible, its raw power and variety has something electric for everyone that likes to rampage. In addition, there are tracks with some clever and memorable hijinks, see 'Voodoo' and 'KKK Bitch.'"

"Think of Body Count as 'grindhouse,' like when a guy runs to his car, he doesn't pull out a gun, he pulls out a rocket launcher," Ice stated.[5] *Body Count*, is steeped in horror, crime drama, action, and blaxploitation, presenting fiction that can show a more complete reality than the news. Body Count's blend of social criticism with grindhouse violence, from the prison drama of "Bowels of the Devil" to the gothic horror of "Voodoo" to the slasher film gore of "Momma's Gotta Die Tonight," marks them as rock fathers of horrorcore, the rap subgenre popularized by artists like Gravediggaz and Ice's Analog Brothers bandmate Kool Keith. "Voodoo" rewrites the long-standing Black horror trope, and racist white anxiety, of a Louisiana voodoo priestess, as well as the slight return of a theme from hard rock's greatest Black pioneer. Ice's performance draws on some of his most novelistic storytelling to create edge of your seat characters, punctuated by Ice's hilarious, pained outbursts as the woman stabs the voodoo doll's eye and cuts off its fingers (a fate that also befalls Ice's character in *Leprechaun 5: In the Hood*). "I really like 'Voodoo,'" says Lamb of God's Randy Blythe. "His

---

[5]*Revolver.* "Body Count 'Carnivore' Q&A with Ice-T." *YouTube*, March 4, 2020, https://youtu.be/Y_5mTKl2ie0.

delivery when she starts hurting him through the voodoo doll is great."

"Hip-hop has always been a vehicle for telling stories about the Black urban experience, but horrorcore goes deeper and darker into the B-movie, slasher nightmare of psychosis, Satanism, cannibalism, mutilations, necrophilia, murder and torture," wrote Leila Taylor in *Darkly: Black History and America's Gothic Soul.* "The classic themes of racism, gang violence, drugs, police brutality, and poverty use the language of horror movies to tell their story."[6]

"The triumph of Ice-T's metal group Body Count was one-upping the mediated and vicarious experience of Eighties thrash, a genre built on the novels of Lovecraft and King, the atrocities of history and the dispatches of TV news," Christopher R. Weingarten wrote for *Rolling Stone's* "100 Greatest Metal Albums of All Time" feature. "Instead, Body Count presented street-level reportage, showing life in contemporary South Central Los Angeles as a house of horrors: nights erupting with the sound of gang warfare ('Body Count'), a prison system devouring Black males ('Bowels of the Devil'), friends ravaged by crack cocaine ('The Winner Loses')—not to mention venom directed at the "stupid, dumb, dick-sucking, bum politicians" blind to it all."[7]

"Ice makes everything different because he's one of the greatest MCs of all time," says Chuck D. "When he takes on

[6]Taylor, Leila. *Darkly: Blackness and America's Gothic Soul.* United States, Repeater, 2019.

[7]Westhoff, Ben. *Original Gangstas: Tupac Shakur, Dr. Dre, Eazy-E, Ice Cube, and the Birth of West Coast Rap.* United States, Hachette Books, 2017.

ugly terrains of noise and shrapnel it's automatically going to come out like nothing else you've ever heard. And then you've got Black cats strumming hard. You can't beat that. When they play a song, they're filling the whole moment."

Body Count draws the Black American experience with horror aesthetics, making listeners squint to find the difference. The band is distinct but never defined, captivating listeners into determining which lyrics are serious or not, daring us to distinguish between the horror stories they're unveiling on record and the ones occurring in America while we listen. "Some of my music is not solution-oriented. Particularly the group Body Count," Ice told *Spin*. "This is the anger, this is the scream from the bottom. Body Count, in a way, should be slightly ignorant—meaning it can't be too intelligent. I want it to be very raw, and sometimes just stupid . . . You'll hear lyrics on the Body Count album, and you'll say, 'Ice-T knows better than that.' But I'm not singing as me."[8]

While maintaining Ice's storytelling bravado, there's little to romanticize in Body Count. There's none of Ice's gangsta rap materialism—the closest he comes to luxury goods are the AK and hand grenades in "Body Count." Ice's domestic life, often a part of his solo albums and music videos, is out of the picture on *Body Count*. The album does retain Ice's licentiousness, feminizing his tribulations and tying his libido to white fears about Black sexuality. "KKK Bitch" shows the band going down south to romp with the Nazi

[8]Woods, Karen. "Police on My Back." *Spin*, September 1992.

master race daughter of a KKK grand wizard, attend a rally in Klan disguise, and end up with a KKK grandchild named "Little Ice-T" (live, Ice sometimes changes it to "Little Ernie C"). "KKK Bitch was real. We toured all through the Bible Belt, and there'd be white girls backstage,"[9] Ice told *Metal Hammer*.

Despite their blunt anti-racism, Body Count could hardly be called "woke." One struggles to think of any record that's both as intellectually progressive and politically incorrect as *Body Count*, attacking racism with a Gwar-like sense of shock humor. Ice's prolonged fake orgasm in "Evil Dick" gets funnier the longer it goes, an unforgettable moment on record and on stage. In "KKK Bitch," Ice lists the indiscriminate types of girls Body Count enjoys, concluding, "If you from Mars, and you got a pussy, we will fuck you." "You ever seen the movie *Blue Velvet*? You know that bit where Dennis Hopper says: 'I'll fuck anything that moves!'? It was that whole attitude," Ice stated. "It's a weird way of breaking down racism. I'm equal opportunities. I think most guys are."[10]

"One thing about rap and metal, there is a lot of humor in it." Ice told *Musician*. "But if you don't see the humor, it'll scare the living shit out of you."[11]

---

[9]Rowley, Scott. "The Record That Stopped the World: The Outrage and the Comedy behind Body Count's Cop Killer." *Metal Hammer*, June 1, 2020, https://www.loudersound.com/features/body-count-story-behind-cop -killer.

[10]Ibid.

[11]Rowland, Mark. "Ice-T: Crap Killer." *Musician*, January 1993, https://www .rocksbackpages.com/library/article/ice-t-crap-killer.

The sex objects in "KKK Bitch" and "Evil Dick," plus the evil women of "Momma's Gotta Die Tonight" and "Voodoo," are not going to placate critics of Ice's sexism, which was often celebrated by male critics for its provocation. "Since the beginning of my career, I have been accused of sexism because I am honest and vocal about the way men perceive women," Ice stated in *The Ice Opinion*. "If women want to be treated equally, earn equal wages, and attain equal status in the workplace, then I'm a feminist."[12] That didn't get him out friendly disagreements with Terry Gross on *Fresh Air* ("I'm not sexist . . . I look at your butt and you look at my butt. I'm sexual.")[13] or Whoopi Goldberg on her late-night show. ("That's a valid complaint. I guess you got to just look at it, if a man is making a record, sometimes men are going to come from a male and slightly chauvinistic approach, and that's just part of it. But when women come back at us, I'm like 'touché.'")[14]

"Body Count is *Seinfeld*! It's all about something but it's all about nothing," laughed Ernie in 2017. "It's the same band that can play 'KKK Bitch' and then turn around and play 'No Lives Matter.'"[15]

[12]Ice-T and Heidi Siegmund Cuda. *The Ice Opinion: Who Gives a Fuck?* United States, St. Martin's Press, 1994.

[13]"Rapper and Actor Ice-T." *Fresh Air* Archive: Interviews with Terry Gross, May 16, 1994, https://freshairarchive.org/segments/rapper-and-actor-ice-t -0.

[14]"90's Throwback: The Whoopi Goldberg Show - Ice-T." *YouTube*, May 1, 2014, https://youtu.be/UImTyRHRT8M.

[15]Bianca. "Conversations with Bianca: Body Count + Bloodlust + Ice-T + Ernie C." May 29, 2017, http://conversationswithbianca.com/2017/05/29/body-count-ernie-c/.

"We were just a band that played the songs that we knew how to write," stated Ernie. "Like the Beach Boys sing about the beach, we sing about the way we grew up."[16] Of course, the Beach Boys, like Body Count, created characters in their songs. While Body Count makes stories like "Cop Killer," "KKK Bitch," "Voodoo," and "Momma's Gotta Die Tonight" vivid for listeners, they're meant to be taken about as literally as non-surfer Brian Wilson writing about beaches he'd never been to in "Surfin' USA." "I always said I wrote 'faction,'" Ice told *Metal Injection*. "I would write factual occurrences put into a fictional story. . . . It's so heavy that it rings real."[17]

"I like 'Momma's Gotta Die Tonight.' That's one of my favorites because that was based off a movie that we liked, *Henry: Portrait of a Serial Killer*," says Sean E. Sean. "We had that movie on loop. So when Ice starts going into what he did with his mom that was just coming off that movie."

"'Momma's Gotta Die Tonight' really was influenced heavy by Rollins Band. You know how Henry Rollins would get into that groove and start talking?" says Ice. "We were just picking up ideas." A lesser vocalist, or even many great

[16]Yoxheimer, Aaron. "Body Count: It's a Survivor." *The Morning Call*, October 5, 2021, https://www.mcall.com/news/mc-xpm-2007-03-31 -3708636-story.html.

[17]Godla, Frank. "Ice T Talks Body Count Fans, What the Grammys Are Really like, the Current State of Racism & More." *Metal Injection*, December 22, 2020, https://metalinjection.net/interviews/ice-t-talks-body-count-fans -what-the-grammys-are-really-like-the-current-state-of-racism-more.

ones, would get drowned by the monologue in "Momma's Gotta Die Tonight," but Ice-T pushes it through with his acting chops. "In this song, I confront the issue of the way Black people from my father's generation view racism. He talked to me about white people differently to the way that I would talk to my son. But there again, I respect what those who grew up in the 1940s and 1950s went through and did to make things better for Blacks," Ice said.[18]

The self-explanatory title and punk Sabbath riffs in "Body Count Anthem" create a top-level hype song, including a "BC" chant that hails the band but also conjures a distinguishing trait of Ice's rap career—he didn't rep gangs. Ice wore both red and blue clothing, while fans debated his true gang affiliation, and the "BC" initials include both Bloods and Crips. The *Body Count* cover figure's dark purplish bandana wasn't giving any clues either, making fans look and listen more closely to try to find out. Later, the rival gangs' "B" and "C" hand signs would be combined in the cover art to Body Count's *Violent Demise* record.

In the unflinching "There Goes the Neighborhood," Ice sometimes draws out the last syllable when he sings the title, while the scared white narrator lashes out at the Black band for being "too hardcore," a subgenre of punk,

---

[18]Rowley, Scott. "The Record That Stopped the World: The Outrage and the Comedy behind Body Count's Cop Killer." *Metal Hammer*, June 1, 2020, https://www.loudersound.com/features/body-count-story-behind-cop-killer.

rap, and pornography to play into the character's fears. It's the word Ice uses most to describe Body Count. "You can't call us metal, cause if we're metal, then what's 'KKK Bitch?' That's punk," Ice stated in 2018. "When we do 'Talk Shit, Get Shot,' and we breakdown, it gets funky. . . . Regardless, it's hardcore."[19]

"I think it's a brilliant song . . . a statement on racism in America where Black people would move into a house, but also it's him as a Black musician, and of course Ernie and them, moving into a realm that is primarily not inhabited, at least not then, by Black musicians," says Blythe.

The song's three-fingered tapping segment was inspired by Eddie Van Halen. "That's still hard to play. We didn't play with it a click, so I think if we would have played with a click it would have made the timing a little different and wouldn't have flowed as easily as it does. I play with a click sometimes and it sounds too technical, too sterile," says Ernie.

"Ernie's riffs were so simple and so rock 'n' roll," says Biafra. "It hit me more like a punk album than a metal album, although then I noticed they were doing shows with Pantera and others . . . but they didn't sound like any other punk bands, either."

"I wouldn't call it lo-fi, but it was not your normal production for either a punk or a metal album. It was just what they came up with on their own in a vacuum," says Biafra. "I don't think there's a dud on that whole record. Not

[19]"Ice-T & Ernie C of Body Count: New Album Carnivore, Longevity, Creative Writing and More 2018." *YouTube*, June 12, 2018, https://youtu.be /LYTZbplJ-LY.

---

just because the lyrics were like nothing any rock band had ever nailed an audience with ever before . . . complete with Sean E. Sean's gun on stage . . . then there was the music, this was brand new. And it scared the shit out of a million times more people than ever hid under their beds because of anything by MDC or Dead Kennedys or Black Flag or anybody else."

"I love that first record because it's so punk rock," says Cavalera. "I think it's the one of the rawest records that's ever been made. . . . 'There Goes the Neighborhood,' 'KKK Bitch.' Some great fucking direct songs on that record."

At risk of hyperbole, listening to *Body Count* today one thinks of those standard music biopics where some frantic exec tells Ray Charles he can't make a country record, or James Brown's bandmates insist that he stick to gospel. Who thought this would work? How does it sound so easy? There had been rap-rock crossovers before, like "Walk This Way" and "Bring the Noise," but those brought two different acts together. This wasn't a rap act using rock-inflected beats, like Run-DMC, and it wasn't a rock band with rapped verses, like the Red Hot Chili Peppers. "We wanted a group that has the attack of Slayer, the impending doom of Sabbath, the drive of Motörhead and groove-oriented, to come up with what I call consumable hardcore music—a record that once you hear it you can sing it. Like what Anthrax does, that power hook. I like being in a show and having a crowd involved," Ice stated.[20] In other interviews, he'd add Venice gang punks

---

[20]Rowland, Mark. "Ice-T: Crap Killer." *Musician*, January 1993, https://www.rocksbackpages.com/library/article/ice-t-crap-killer.

Suicidal Tendencies to the equation, describing them as "the first gangster-based rock band."[21]

As one would expect from an Ice-T-fronted hardcore band, Body Count are more theatrical than nearly all their punk or metal contemporaries. But after years of stating that his rap records weren't written for dancing ("We intentionally used beats that you couldn't dance to, because you're supposed to sit back and listen to me kick game."[22]), Body Count wrote a danceable record that retained Ice's lyrical prowess. More specifically, Body Count wrote a mosh pit classic, a slam-dancing masterpiece that matches the crowd's energy with the band's. "For anybody who's ever performed, playing in front of a mosh pit is the most exciting shit in the world," Ice stated.[23] "Our objective is to crush people in that pit. We don't have a good show unless an ambulance shows up."[24]

"Ice-T's lyrics about the hate-hate relationship between police and young Blacks have a stomach-churning immediacy," Greg Kot reviewed *Body Count* in the *Chicago Tribune*. "On the stereotype-bashing 'There Goes the Neighborhood,' the humor, message and music coalesce

[21] Ice-T and Douglas Century. *Ice: A Memoir of Gangster Life and Redemption-from South Central to Hollywood.* United States, Random House Publishing Group, 2011.

[22] "Ice-T." Red Bull Music Academy, https://www.redbullmusicacademy.com /lectures/ice-t.

[23] *Revolver.* "Body Count 'Carnivore' Q&A with Ice-T." *YouTube*, March 4, 2020, https://youtu.be/Y_5mTKl2ie0.

[24] Viera, Ralph. "Body Count - Compilation." *YouTube*, April 19, 2017, https://youtu.be/JpZd6uTDMPI.

brilliantly, and Body Count proves equally adept at working Slayer's speed-metal turf ('Bowels of the Devil,' 'Voodoo') or delving into King's X-style melodicism ('The Winner Loses,' 'C Note')."[25]

The latter two songs were the record's only cuts written entirely by Ernie C. The ominous instrumental "C Note," sharing a name with both its author and Iceberg Slim novel slang for a $100 bill, delivers a beautiful, measured composition that's nonetheless short enough to appeal to anybody who was hoping for a punk record. "I was in the studio myself playing on top of these, like, four chords," remembered Ernie. "The guitar almost sounded like it was crying."[26]

The mournful, partly-acoustic "The Winner Loses," the record's sole power ballad, received a single and a music video edit, no doubt in part due to being the record's least hostile song. Its anti-drug lyrics and video might've helped establish Body Count as role models, and its musicians as versatile players, were it not overshadowed by another song. But the fans knew better, and from the start, Body Count weren't going to be pigeonholed. "Ice always says, 'Ernie likes making these big drama songs,'" says Ernie.

[25]Kot, Greg. "Body Count *Body Count*." *Chicago Tribune*, August 10, 2021, https://www.chicagotribune.com/news/ct-xpm-1992-05-21-9202150441 -story.html.

[26]Angle, Brad. "Firestorm: Body Count's Ice-T and Ernie C Look Back on the Making of – and Reaction to – Their Polarizing Self-Titled 1992 Debut Album." *Guitar World*, June 2022.

"Moose's playing was different. He'd add extra notes on the bass that you normally wouldn't get in rock 'n' roll. A song like 'The Winner Loses' he's playing all kinds of harmonics," Ernie recalled. "And the drums were straight R&B."[27]

As a guitarist, Ernie's tones harden and enhance Ice's vocals. Ernie rips with a DIY flavor that's harder to imitate than it sounds, switching between a Moser, a Les Paul, and an Ovation inspired by Ernie's jazz fusion influences, like Al Di Meola and John McLaughlin. "Ice makes my playing digestible. Sometimes, if you're just writing a record with guitar players, it'll be like a Steve Vai record with notes all over the place. Ice makes it easy for people to relate to," Ernie told MusicRadar.[28]

"He's a weird mix of all kinds of cool shit, from Hendrix to some metal guys that I don't know that he references," McKagan describes Ernie. "He's definitely got his own niche. There's no other guitar player who plays like him, and songwriting-wise I think they're the king of the breakdown."

Other than "C Note" and "The Winner Loses," the record stays pretty much on its punk-metal track. But *Body Count* never feels limited or monotonous. It's a focused, seamless blend. Body Count have more than enough to hone in on—they earned critical acclaim for attacking bigotry, but listeners came away from the record seeing racism, police

---

[27]Ibid.

[28]Chamberlain, Rich. "Ernie C Talks Bloodlust, Producing Black Sabbath and 25 Years of Body Count." MusicRadar, March 9, 2017, https://www .musicradar.com/news/ernie-c-talks-bloodlust-black-sabbath-and-25-years -of-body-count.

brutality, white supremacy, classism, and institutional racism all differentiated in songs like "Body Count," "Bowels of the Devil," "There Goes the Neighborhood," "KKK Bitch," and "Momma's Gotta Die Tonight." In the record's final interlude, "Out in the Parking Lot," Ice takes his most concrete swipe at the police yet, dedicating the next song to the LAPD.

Ice riffed on "Out in the Parking Lot" live, the cheers getting louder from the fans who realized what song was coming up next. Sometimes he dared the cops at the venue to arrest the fans who sang along. When Ice lists the reasons cops might have assaulted you, for having long hair, listening to loud music, or being the wrong color, the crowd starts to clamor.

From Ernie's breakneck opening riff and Ice's yell, "Cop Killer" crushes taboos and pushes anti-police sentiments further than "Fuck tha Police" or "911 is a Joke." That wouldn't matter if Body Count didn't also write a landmark of metal and punk that has never been equaled, an Americanized D-beat progression armed with a gunshot percussion hook fifteen years before "Paper Planes." It packs two guitar solos and a rhythm section breakdown into an infectious four-minute punk song. Critics compared "Cop Killer" to the classic "Stagger Lee," and the song's defenders would point out that it doesn't romanticize its killer more than Woody Guthrie eulogized Jesse James or Pretty Boy Floyd. Yet no comparisons sufficiently captured the path "Cop Killer" was forging in American folklore.

"'Cop Killer' was basically 'authority killer,'" said Ice. "I hate bullies and racists and people who take advantage of their position. Whether that's a cop or your boss at work or the guy on the block."[29]

"It's a protest song with a bit of punk influence," says current Body Count guitarist Juan of the Dead. "A very simple song with a massive message."

"Emotionally, that album really seemed to fit the times in terms of what young Black people like myself were feeling. We were angry at the cops, we had been harassed by the cops. And I think that when *Body Count* came out, it was like, 'Yes, this is the soundtrack to our internalized anger,'" remembers Dawes.

"To me this was an urban twist on what other heavy bands were doing," said Ice. "We'd toured with Napalm Death and Cannibal Corpse, and they had songs with far worse sentiments than 'Cop Killer.' But you know what the difference was? You couldn't hear their lyrics, whereas with me you got every word."[30]

[29]Mörat. "Body Count: The Story behind Cop Killer." *Kerrang!*, February 28, 2020, https://www.kerrang.com/body-count-the-story-behind-cop-killer.

[30]Dome, Malcolm. "Body Count: The Story behind the Debut Album." *Metal Hammer*, August 2, 2006, https://www.loudersound.com/features/body-count-the-story-behind-body-count-album.

7

"Body Count's in the house."

"What you're listening to right now is the new Body Count album," Ice-T says in live performance footage. "It'll be in the stores March 31, it'll be banned March 32, you've gotta get it quick."[1]

The album was titled *Cop Killer* and served with a menacing, comic book-style cover depicting a strapped, muscle-bound man with the title tattooed on his chest, described by Halili as "an Ice and Halili collaboration 100%."[2] While preparing for the album's release, Warner's head of promotion Russ Thyret, a policeman's son, expressed

[1]Viera, Ralph. "Body Count—Compilation." *YouTube*, April 19, 2017, https://youtu.be/JpZd6uTDMPI.

[2]Hart, Sam. "Visual Artist Dave Halili Talks about His Work on Body Count's Iconic Debut Release." *Metal Injection*, July 7, 2021, https://metalinjection.net/editorials/back-in-the-day/visual-artist-dave-halili-talks-about-his-work-on-body-counts-debut-release-the-iconic-cop-killer-cover-art.

some mild concerns about the last song on *Cop Killer*. Execs discussed the song but didn't really consider removing it, and Ice eased any concerns by changing the album title to *Body Count* while keeping the song. The cover art stayed, and the liner notes included a corporate disclaimer: "Neither Sire Records nor Warner Bros. Records are responsible for anything in connection with their merchandise."[3]

"It's kind of the art of being hardcore. Sometimes you got to seem like you compromise and still get your way," Ice stated on *Rockline*. "The name of the album is *Cop Killer*. I know, regardless of what they want to call it, we know it."[4] On *Headbangers Ball*, he promoted the album as *Cop Killer*.

That March, promotional Body Count CDs were sent to radio stations in little black body bags, including the humorously titled *The Radio EP*, featuring edited versions of *Body Count* songs. "Early in rap, I wouldn't do edited versions," says Ice, a self-proclaimed "album artist."[5] "Even today they're like 'Okay, can we do radio edits of the new album?' and I hate doing it," he adds. "But now I look back, and I think I would have had a lot more success if I had just made clean versions along with the hard version."

[3]Body Count. *Body Count*, Sire Records, 1992.

[4]Viera, Ralph. "Body Count on *Rockline*." *YouTube*, April 18, 2017, https://youtu.be/BkM2x51WVSk.

[5]McQueen, Gregg. "An Interview with Ice-T from Body Count: Cold Metal." *The Aquarian*, January 3, 2018, https://www.theaquarian.com/2014/07/30/an-interview-with-ice-t-from-body-count-cold-metal/.

"My daughter brought one of her Barbie dolls to school in that body bag for show and tell," says Ernie. "That involved a parent teacher conference."

Body Count's debut single "There Goes the Neighborhood" also featured Halili's artwork, an illustration of Black hands in cuffs shown from the backside. For a video, the band enlisted veteran director Matt Mahurin, whose foreboding, black-and-white style had recently graced Metallica's "The Unforgiven." "We knew Matt Mahurin was the shit because he had done the Metallica shit," says Ice. "He had this back story of us coming into the suburbs and the real fear, which is the Black man with the white girl."

The video was filmed in Compton, with what Mahurin describes as "run and gun style," starting in "a house 'graveyard'—a big lot filled with condemned houses that had been removed from their original build sites . . . . The plan was to start at the house graveyard, then work our way out of the inner city, on to Beverly Hills shops, and finally ending up in an upper-class suburb. We would improvise as we went along to follow the young Black man's journey."

The video ends with a Black man planting a burning upside-down guitar in a suburban yard. "A not-so-subtle message that Body Count was here to stay," says Mahurin.

"By having a new band's first record get on MTV, especially Body Count, that was tremendous for us," says Ice. "That video launched the band."

In an unprecedented sweep, "There Goes the Neighborhood" was added to MTV shows *Headbangers*

Ball, Yo! MTV Raps, 120 Minutes, and *Buzz Bin.* An MTV contest was planned to give away Body Count's music video equipment. Ice filmed an episode of *Rockumentary* for the channel. "There Goes the Neighborhood" even earned Body Count the ultimate MTV honor, getting chanted and air-guitared by Beavis and Butt-head. The duo chanted it on Season Two's "For Better or Verse" and on Season Four's "Right On," a music censorship-themed episode featuring a conservative TV host–turned presidential candidate who promises to "make this country great again." It aired in 1994.

"When Ronald Reagan used to talk about the 'good old days' and George Bush and Dan Quayle harped on 'family values,' they weren't appealing to me or anybody who's Black," Ice stated. "The tradition of America is to own slaves. Tradition. The good old days. Oh, you mean when I was on the back of the bus? When I couldn't drink from your water fountain or eat in your restaurants?"[6]

Modern-day Body Count producer Will Putney remembers catching "There Goes the Neighborhood" on MTV. "It was the scariest thing that existed in music to me," says Putney. "It combined everything I thought was aggressive about rock music with everything that was scary to a young white kid about hip-hop in this one package. I loved it immediately because it was massively entertaining at the same time, and it was such an anti-everything record to the life I had."

[6]Ice-T and Heidi Siegmund Cuda. *The Ice Opinion: Who Gives a Fuck?* St. Martin's Press, 1994.

Ice' and Ernie booked an appearance on MTV's *Rockline*, in which Ice described the "There Goes the Neighborhood" video to interviewer Martha Quinn as "one that you would want to ban but couldn't ban." "Work that edge," Ice added.

Ice turned a story about a canceled Body Count performance at the Whisky a Go Go into some of the most enthralling punk notoriety since Bad Brains were banned in DC. "We got banned in Los Angeles, which made us feel, 'Hey, we're good!'" he enthused. "The word got out that it was Ice-T in the band, so you were getting my crowd showing up to small venues that are used to only handling 500 people. The LA Sheriff's Department said, 'No, this band can't play.'"[7] "Hot Rod" Long confirms Body Count getting served with a safety bond for police protection, which Ice offered to pay before the Whisky show was canceled by owner Mario Maglieri under LASD pressure. The show was moved to the sold-out Spice on Hollywood Boulevard.

"That made us even more the band to see," says Ernie. "They didn't let us play at the Roxy or the Whisky or nowhere else on the Sunset Strip. . . . They tried to associate Ice with rap. There wasn't a rap show. It was gonna be a rock show."

Ice and Ernie took questions from callers, which the bandmates handled with their usual charm. One caller raved about *Body Count*, praising the record's messages, humor, and musicianship, before bringing up the 1990 Judas Priest "subliminal message" trial, in which two Nevada parents sued the band for allegedly inspiring two young men to

[7]Viera, Ralph. "Body Count on *Rockline*." *YouTube*, April 18, 2017, https://youtu.be/BkM2x51WVSk.

shoot themselves in suicide pact (a judge dismissed the case). "How would you react to a 14-year-old kid who listens to the song 'Cop Killer' and went out and shot a cop as a result of it, and went back and said, 'Oh, I did it because Body Count said to?'" the caller asked.

"I say a lot of things, even in the rap that shouldn't be taken too seriously," Ice responded. "If a kid were to do that, then I'd deal with that situation when it came up. But hopefully, if anybody's out there watching, don't go shoot no police, and don't kill your mother, it's a record, dude. These are characters. The cop killer, he's a fantasy character who's decided that he could not take police brutality any longer . . . if you can just maintain some of the anger without taking the whole entire step out, you'll get the point across."[8]

Body Count shipped around 300,000 copies. It charted lower and sold slower than *O.G. Original Gangster*. Many rap fans and metalheads, even on the cutting edge of extreme music, did not know what to make of Body Count. Distributors and critics didn't know how to classify them, describing Ice's performance as "rapping" when it had more in common with the hardcore bark of frontmen like Henry Rollins. "It's a rock album with a rap mentality," Ice-T described *Body Count* in *Rolling Stone*. "This album's mentality is a progressive mentality against racism. It's hate against hate, you know. It's

[8]Ibid.

anger. It's not necessarily answers, it's anger with the same force of their hate."[9]

"The PMRC and its ilk ought to be grateful for *Body Count*," stated the magazine's J. D. Considine review, "since it provides the porn patrol with the equivalent of one-stop shopping." The review cited "tunes that make N.W.A. seem like the Patrolman's Benevolence Association" and "the campy good humor of prime Alice Cooper." Still, the critics who appreciated the record's humor knew Body Count were a band to take seriously. "Body Count offers the sort of sonic intensity parental groups fear even more than four-letter words. And that's no joke," Considine concluded.[10]

"They didn't know what to do with Body Count, because there was no category," Ice remembered. "There wasn't anything similar to us, so what do you call it?"[11]

"Body Count wasn't supposed to be a big deal at all. We originally just set out to sell 50,000 records like the Ramones or the Dead Kennedys," recalled Ernie. [12]

"They were so fucking important. And they were so dismissed from the metal magazines. It's like they didn't want

---

[9]Light, Alan. "Ice-T: The *Rolling Stone* Interview." *Rolling Stone*, August 20, 1992.

[10]Considine, J. D. "*Body Count*." *Rolling Stone*, May 14, 1992.

[11]Dawes, Laina. "Body Count's Ice-T Talks Shit but Does the Shooting." *Decibel Magazine*, June 5, 2014, https://www.decibelmagazine.com/2014/06 /05/body-count-s-ice-t-talks-shit-but-does-the-shooting/.

[12]Yoxheimer, Aaron. "Body Count: It's a Survivor." *The Morning Call*, October 5, 2021, https://www.mcall.com/news/mc-xpm-2007-03-31 -3708636-story.html.

to say, 'How dare a Black rapper put together a metal band?'" says Cuda. "So instead they were bashing the technique, or the guitar here, or whatever."

After about two-thirds of the shipped records sold, unsold copies started returning to Warner Music. "That's a successful record," says Klein. "It's not over the top, but it's good, and it's good enough to do a second record as well. So we were happy, and we started taking returns from the store . . . a normal thing."

On April 28, 1992, less than one month after *Body Count*'s release, four Crips and Bloods sets successfully negotiated the Watts truce, a years-in-the making ceasefire (and inspiration for Ice's *Home Invasion* song "Gotta Lotta Love"). The day after the truce, a predominately white jury acquitted the officers involved in the Rodney King beating, and the week's subsequent riots and uprising led to a reported sixty-three deaths, over 2,383 injured, over 12,000 arrests, and over $1 billion in property damage, leaving tens of thousands out of work and passing the Watts riots to mark the deadliest and most expensive civil unrest in American history.

Compton's Stevie Wonder-owned radio station, KJLH, broke its all-music format to cover the story and interviewed Ice on May 2. Ice also spoke to reporters over his car phone from the frontlines. When a KTTV Los Angeles anchor asked Ice-T to do something to "stop the riots," Ice refused. "It hurts me to see my neighborhood going up like this," he said. "At the same time, I can't honestly say that if I didn't have this money in my pocket, and I wasn't who I was, that I wouldn't be there too."[13]

On April 30, Mayor Bradley, a former policeman, asked residents to stay home and watch the *Cosby* series finale, pleading, "Maybe you'll hear him make a final appeal on his show."[14] Cosby himself had sent a taped message to KNBC earlier that day urging viewers to obey curfew and watch his show. Later that evening, the station's news anchors announced eighteen confirmed deaths in local violence right before segueing to anchor Jess Marlow introducing "a welcome change of pace" and "a breath of fresh air in a sometimes crazy and chaotic world much like we saw today," reiterating the Mayor's request to "stay home, stay off the streets and watch *The Cosby Show*."[15] One year earlier, Body Count had introduced themselves on *O.G. Original Gangster*, with Ice stating that reality is not like *The Cosby Show*.

[13]Charnas, Dan. *The Big Payback: The History of the Business of Hip-Hop.* United States, Penguin Publishing Group, 2011.

[14]*Let It Fall: Los Angeles 1982–1992.* Directed by John Ridley, ABC Studios, 2017.

[15]"KNBC Interrupts La Riot Coverage for Cosby Show Finale." *YouTube,* September 15, 2011, https://youtu.be/KX1Npoy0atU.

8
"Stop the car right here."

That May, Dallas senior corporal police officer Glenn White, who edited the Dallas Police Association's monthly newsletter, *The Shield*, was approached by Sgt. Ron Rose with a concern for the next issue. Rose had photocopied a lyrics sheet from an album one of his teen daughter's friends had brought over. White read the lyrics.

"New Rap Song Encourages Killing Police Officers" was a headline in the May issue of *The Shield*. "I urge you to BOYCOTT any and all Time Warner products and movies until such time as they have recalled this tape," wrote White.[1] Warner Bros. Records President Lenny Waronker's contact info was printed at the bottom, and the newsletter was sent to thousands of subscribers throughout Texas.

---

[1]Charnas, Dan. *The Big Payback: The History of the Business of Hip-Hop.* United States, Penguin Publishing Group, 2011.

Days after the story's publication, a Corpus Christi police officer forwarded the article to a reporter from local paper the *Caller-Times*, who then called Ron DeLord, a former Texas cop who had cofounded CLEAT, representing about 12,000 Texas police officers and serving as the organization's first president since 1977. "Dallas wasn't affiliated with us, but I knew Glenn. And he called me about having heard this song and they wanted to do something about it," says DeLord. "We said, 'Well, Time Warner owns Six Flags, Six Flags is in Arlington. Let's just do a press conference up in Arlington and make it about this,' and it got massive press. It just took off, had legs."

DeLord booked the press conference at Six Flags while White received an *Entertainment Tonight* crew in Dallas and was flown by CBS to New York for interviews. CLEAT issued the boycott on June 10, announced by DeLord the next day at Six Flags with White standing nearby. The statement demanded apologies from Ice-T and Time Warner, called for the song's removal, and for Ice-T to make a million-dollar donation to a community services program by the July 16 Time Warner shareholders meeting. Otherwise, the police would pressure their pension funds to divest themselves of Time Warner stock.

"We were singing 'Cop Killer,' really for like a year before the controversy hit," says Ice. "Prior to us, there's a punk band called Millions of Dead Cops, and Black Flag was always talking shit about the police, so I felt the police were a fair target."

Ice still thought the story would blow over when Time Warner flew him to New York for the conglomerate's

Executive Forum in the Time Life Building, featuring New York hip-hop icon Fab Five Freddy in conversation with Ice-T. Ice brushed off the controversy near the start and enjoyed an engaging and informative discussion about music, politics, and culture. That night Ice joined several execs for a swanky Manhattan dinner.

"Lenny Waronker called me up and said, 'Hey, what do you know about this?' He showed me a stack of letters he had gotten, all of which said more or less the same thing. It was just a deluge of letters that were clearly the result of an organized campaign," says Merlis.

DeLord mailed hundreds of information packets containing Time Warner names, products, and contact info, with an invitation to the shareholders meeting, to police and sheriff organizations all over the country. "We intend to boycott any and all products, movies and amusement parks, such as your Six Flags, that are owned and operated by Time Warner," read a protest letter sent by thousands of cops, with variations, to Warner Bros.[2]

"The phone started to ring with the media talking about this Ice-T record advocating the murder of police. I said 'First of all, it's not an Ice-T record. It's a Body Count record,'" says Merlis. "To suggest that it advocated that is on par with suggesting that Randy Newman's 'Short People' advocated

---

[2]Royko, Mike. "The Profit Motive Lifts the Lid on Garbage." *Baltimore Sun*, June 30, 1992, https://www.baltimoresun.com/news/bs-xpm-1992-06-30 -1992182163-story.html.

the murder of people who were not of great height. If you take art literally, you run the risk of appearing stupid."

Barely any publications got the artist or genre right, with even the *New York Times*, Associated Press, CNN, and MTV misidentifying "Cop Killer" as Ice-T's rap song. Some sources incorrectly reported that the record had sold millions, or that "Cop Killer" was featured in Warner film *Batman Returns*. "They always said, 'It's a rap record.' It wasn't a rap record. That record is as metal or as punk as you can get," says Ernie.

"If you say a rock record came out called 'Cop Killer,' a lot of the white people with power would say, 'Well, I like Aerosmith. I like Fleetwood Mac. Maybe I'd like this song,'" Ice told an interviewer. "But if you say 'rap,' 'That means niggers and I don't like it.'"[3]

"During the course of that time, that's all we did," says Merlis. "As a corporate communications officer for the company there was no time to do anything else . . . it was really an impediment to our marketing the rest of the catalog."

"A lot of people demanded that we pull the video and single for the song 'Cop Killer,' when in fact there never existed a video or single of 'Cop Killer.' People were told to do this, and were given our number and went to town without ever having heard the record."

"It was unrelenting, those calls and threats kept coming in," says Stewart. "This is pre-email, right? It wasn't like you had an unlimited amount of inbox. I think we had four phone lines, and they could all be occupied at the same time. . . . I

---

[3]"Ice-T Controversy during the LA Riots." *YouTube*, November 29, 2013, https://youtu.be/UxC3IU4BHVk.

don't think there'd been an artist controversy to that scale, ever."

The building's phones, mailroom, and fax machine were flooded with threats. Some hate mail was addressed to "Lenny 'Cop Killer' Waronker." An unnamed exec was called a "nigger-loving Jew" in an anonymous phone call death threat.[4] "They found this strangely-packaged box in the mail room, and they alerted security," says Merlis. "They called the bomb squad that blew it up and then we looked at the remnants and it was somebody's tape."

"Lenny Waronker got about 500 death threats, not only to him but to his children," Ice stated. "They never threatened me, it was like, 'Ice-T, we know why you did it. But you big white corporation, how could you be associated with those niggers?'"[5]

"The police really got crazy about it, and they started calling in bomb threats at Warner Bros. I know this because one of the guys at the Burbank police was an old friend of mine and a real pal, and he warned me what was happening," says Klein. "They would call in a bomb threat and make everyone leave the building . . . hundreds of people in the parking lot while they would go through the building looking for bombs which didn't exist, which they knew because they called in

[4]*EW* staff. "Is Ice-T's 'Cop Killer' Legal?" *Entertainment Weekly*, August 14, 1992, https://ew.com/article/1992/08/14/ice-ts-cop-killer-legal/.

[5]Rowland, Mark. "Ice-T: Crap Killer." *Musician*, January 1993, https://www.rocksbackpages.com/library/article/ice-t-crap-killer.

the threat themselves," he adds. "That's a little-known fact by the way. I've haven't talked about that."

By promising that Body Count lyrics were too obscene to print, readers assumed the worst. "Cop Killer" was rarely played or transcribed publicly, the music and lyrics kept it off the radio, and it was never promoted with a single or video. People needed to buy *Body Count* to hear it, and most of Body Count's detractors didn't want to do that. The most printed excerpt, "I got my 12-gauge sawed off/I got my headlights turned off/I'm 'bout to bust some shots off/I'm 'bout to dust some cops off," was one of the only stanzas with no profanity.

The story filled segments of *World News Tonight* with Peter Jennings, *NBC Nightly News* with Tom Brokaw, and CNN's *Moneyline* with Lou Dobbs. Rush Limbaugh, who in June enjoyed dinner and an overnight stay at the White House which included President Bush personally carrying Limbaugh's bags to the Lincoln bedroom, labeled Ice-T's fans "savages and the people who beat up [white LA riots victim] Reginald Denny."[6] But the first White House response to the song came from Vice President Dan Quayle, who'd been using buzzwords like "family values," "corporate responsibility," and "rap" on the Bush-Quayle reelection campaign trail. Quayle found an ideal target for the party's platform.

"I am outraged at the fact that Time Warner, a major corporation, is making money off a record called 'Cop Killer' that suggests it is okay to kill cops," Quayle stated, in a boycott

---

[6]Pollack, Phyllis. "Uninformed Media Serve Ice-T Bashers' Aims." *Billboard*, July 11, 1992.

endorsement that became a staple of his campaign speeches.[7] "The problem is that records like 'Cop Killer' do have an impact on the streets—the wrong impact."[8]

That week, several major record store chains, including Trans World, Super Club, Sound Warehouse, Camelot, Hastings, and Musicland, all announced they were removing *Body Count* from their shelves, dropping the record from at least 1,500 stores. In Greensboro, North Carolina, retailers removed the album when local police told managers they would not respond to emergency calls from the store if they continued to stock the album.[9] "We did not want to be associated with the blunt message expressed in the lyrics," stated Trans World senior VP Jeffrey Jones.[10]

Ice's first public comments on the controversy came on June 18 at a press conference before his keynote speech at the New Music Seminar, an annual music industry meeting at the Times Square Marriott Marquis. "At no point do I go out and say, 'Let's do it.' I'm singing in the first person as a

[7]Devroy, Ann. "The Race for President: Bush Covers Quayle's Tune on Anti-Police Rap Lyrics." *The Washington Post*, June 30, 1992.

[8]Philips, Chuck. "Cover Story: The Uncivil War: The Battle between the Establishment and Supporters of Rap Music Reopens Old Wounds of Race and Class." *Los Angeles Times*, July 19, 1992.

[9]Austin, Joe, and Michael Nevin Willard. *Generations of Youth: Youth Cultures and History in Twentieth-Century America*. United States, New York University Press, 1998.

[10]The Associated Press. "Rapper Ice-T Defends Song against Spreading Boycott (Published 1992)." *The New York Times*, June 19, 1992, https://www.nytimes.com/1992/06/19/arts/rapper-ice-t-defends-song-against-spreading-boycott.html.

character who is fed up with police brutality. I ain't never killed no cop. I felt like it a lot of times. But I never did it . . . that's called a poetic license, and obviously these ignorant pigs don't know nothing about music."[11]

"If the cops got a problem, let them come after me, not Time Warner. They can't boycott me. They don't buy my albums," Ice told reporters.[12] "If you believe that I'm a cop killer, you believe David Bowie is an astronaut."[13] Ice appeared on panels throughout the weekend and co-hosted the seminar's benefit showcase, "Music People United for AIDS Relief."

Despite a growing number of major retailers refusing to sell it, *Body Count* sales surged. A *Hollywood Reporter* story noted "a tripling of *Body Count* album sales in the Lone Star state," including a reported 370 percent leap in Houston, where CLEAT initiated the boycott.[14] "There were no more returns coming in. Instead, the orders started like spiking like mad," says Klein. "Suddenly a record that had sold about 200,000 doubled in sales and then kept going."

[11]Viera, Ralph. "Ice T / Body Count—Cop Killer Controversy." *YouTube*, April 17, 2017, https://youtu.be/AAouKLtnSFw.

[12]The Associated Press. "Rapper Ice-T Defends Song against Spreading Boycott (Published 1992)." *The New York Times*, June 19, 1992, https://www.nytimes.com/1992/06/19/arts/rapper-ice-t-defends-song-against-spreading-boycott.html.

[13]Turner, Will, and Metcalf, Josephine. *Rapper, Writer, Pop-Cultural Player: Ice-T and the Politics of Black Cultural Production*. United Kingdom, Taylor & Francis, 2016.

[14]Layne, Barry. "Quayle, Black Cops Blast 'Killer.'" *The Hollywood Reporter*, June 22, 1992.

"Of course sales increased—I bought one myself," stated DeLord. "We don't care if they sell a million more copies because of our protest. That's not the point. You have to speak out against this sometime. If not now, when? How bad will the next album Time Warner produces be?"[15]

On June 25, the *Wall Street Journal* ran an editorial titled "Why We Won't Withdraw 'Cop Killer,'" by Gerald Levin, calling the song "a shout of pain and protest" that "shares a long history with rock and other forms of urban music" and had "been distorted by politicians on both sides of the aisle into a straw man." "Cutting and running would be the surest and safest way to put the controversy behind us and get on with our business. But in the long run it would be a destructive precedent. It would be a signal to all the artists and journalists inside and outside Time Warner that if they wish to be heard, then they must tailor their minds and souls to fit the reigning orthodoxies," wrote Levin. "The future of our country of our country—indeed of our world—is contained in the commitment to truth and free expression, in the refusal to run away."[16]

Rep. Maxine Waters sent a letter to Levin thanking him for "taking a stand against the right-wing forces that would

---

[15]Philips, Chuck. "'Cop Killer' Controversy Spurs Ice-T Album Sales: Pop Music: 'We Don't Care If They Sell a Million More Copies Because of Our Protest,' Says the President of Combined Law Enforcement Assn. of Texas." *Los Angeles Times*, June 18, 1992.

[16]Levin, Gerald. "Why We Won't Withdraw 'Cop Killer.'" *Wall Street Journal,* June 24, 1992.

deny us all our constitutional rights."[17] Organizations like the ACLU and Norman Lear's People for the American Way joined in support, and several artists, including Anthrax, Beastie Boys, Sonic Youth, Ministry, and Gwar, supported the group in a *Daily Variety* ad headlined, "How does Dan Quayle Spell Censorship? I-C-E-T."[18] Executive Director Ronald Hampton of the Washington-based National Black Police Association, the only police group that denounced the King verdict and the "Cop Killer" boycott, stated that police groups did not show "the same level of outrage when Rodney King was brutally beaten by four Los Angeles police officers." "Artists have always expressed their opinions about social conditions in music. Ice-T's work is in the same tradition," Hampton said. "He's responding to a very real issue that affects many Americans, especially Blacks and Latinos."[19]

DeLord remembers the *WSJ* editorial as Levin's misstep. "The corporation has no free speech rights. Ice-T does. The corporation is not a person," says DeLord. "We were not going to be baited into arguing about the right of Ice-T to say whatever in the heck he wants to say . . . . Time Warner,

---

[17]Morris, Chris, et al. Count Rises on Dealer 'Body Count' Ban: Camelot, Hastings Bow Out Amid Rising Debate. *Billboard*, July 18, 1992.

[18]George, Iestyn. "Ice Fought the Law . . ." *New Musical Express*, August 8, 1992.

[19]Philips, Chuck. "'Cop Killer' Controversy Spurs Ice-T Album Sales: Pop Music: 'We Don't Care If They Sell a Million More Copies Because of Our Protest,' Says the President of Combined Law Enforcement Assn. of Texas." *Los Angeles Times*, June 18, 1992.

as big and as smart as they are took the bait, and then they couldn't sustain that."

"One cop was telling me that the record scares him. And I'm like, well, maybe you should be scared. Because I'm afraid. I'm afraid because some police are way out of control," stated Ice. "There's a point where a cop pulls you out of that car and starts abusing you or beating on you and at that moment he is no longer within the law."[20]

In increasingly divided times, hating Body Count seemed like a rare issue prominent Democrats and Republicans could agree on. In June, sixty congressmen (fifty-seven Republicans and three Democrats), including Republican Party leaders Bob Michel and Newt Gingrich, signed a letter to Time Warner Vice President Jeanette Lerman expressing "our deep sense of outrage" over the "vile and despicable" record. "We believe that your decision to disseminate these despicable lyrics advocating the murder of police officers is unconscionable," read the letter.[21] Senators Alphonse D'Amato [R-NY], Lloyd Bentsen [D-TX], and Daniel Patrick Moynihan [D-NY] all withdrew from appearances in upcoming Warner Bros. political comedy *Dave* in protest. Republican presidential candidate Pat Buchanan insisted

---

[20]Philips, Chuck. "Cover Story: 'Arnold Schwarzenegger Blew Away Dozens of Cops as the Terminator. but I Don't Hear Anybody Complaining.': A Q & A with Ice-T about Rock, Race and the 'Cop Killer' Furor." *Los Angeles Times*, July 19, 1992.

[21]Thomas-Lester, Avis, and Marylou Tousignant. "Reaction to Ice-T Song Heats Up: 60 Congressmen Join Complaint." *The Washington Post*, June 25, 1992.

the Los Angeles "mob" came, in part, "out of rock concerts where rap music celebrates raw lust and cop-killing."[22] Alabama Governor Guy Hunt called for "an urgent Father's Day request" statewide ban on the album, in a statement to the press and letters sent to all other US governors calling to ban the record as well.[23] His office denied that the statement was timed to distract from a grand jury considering ethics charges against Hunt the next day. (Hunt was indicted, convicted, and forced to resign by April 1993.)

New York governor Mario Cuomo called Body Count "Ugly, destructive and disgusting."[24] Democratic presidential nominee Bill Clinton let spokesperson Avis LaVelle state, "The governor has expressed concerns about the hate and violence that has been articulated in some of this music. That record is not exempt from those concerns. . . . He is not advocating curtailing free-speech rights but is advocating greater responsibility on the part of the artists."[25] That summer, Clinton chose Tennessee's Senator Al Gore, husband of anti-rap advocate Tipper, as his running mate.

---

[22]Buchanan, Pat. "Buchanan Calls for Winning Back 'Soul of America.'" *Los Angeles Times*, May 28, 1992.

[23]Times Staff. "Governors Urged to Fight Album." *Tampa Bay Times*, June 22, 1992, https://www.tampabay.com/archive/1992/06/22/governors-urged-to-fight-album/.

[24]Light, Alan. "Ice-T: The *Rolling Stone* Interview." *Rolling Stone*, August 20, 1992.

[25]Morris, Chris, et al. "Bush, New LAPD Chief, NRA Assail Body Count; Cops to Sell TW Stock." *Billboard*, July 11, 1992.

Tipper's PMRC co-founder Susan Baker was married to Bush's Secretary of State James Baker.

On June 29, President George H. W. Bush was in New York campaigning for Senator D'Amato's reelection, speaking to the New York Drug Enforcement Administration. "I stand against those who use films, or records, or television, or video games to glorify killing law enforcement officers. It is sick," Bush stated, drawing applause. "It is wrong for any company—I don't care how noble the name of the company—to issue records that approve of killing law enforcement officers."[26]

It was the first time in history a sitting US president publicly condemned a music industry artist. Bush, an NRA Life Member at the time (he resigned in 1995), had earlier that year campaigned in New Hampshire with his friend and supporter Arnold Schwarzenegger, whose most famous character had killed and maimed several police officers onscreen in *Terminator 2: Judgment Day*, 1991's highest-grossing film. While promoting the film, director James Cameron liked to note that the tape of the Rodney King beating also contained scenes from the set of *Terminator 2*, filmed blocks away from taper George Holliday's Lake View Terrace home. "That, to me, is the most amazing irony considering that the LAPD are strongly represented in *Terminator 2* as being a dehumanized force," said Cameron.[27]

[26]Devroy, Ann. "The Race for President: Bush Covers Quayle's Tune on Anti-Police Rap Lyrics." *The Washington Post*, June 30, 1992.

[27]Klimek, Chris. "In the '90s, *Terminator*'s Ultimate Evil Took the Form of a Cop. in 2019, It's the Border Patrol." *Slate*, November 4, 2019, https://slate

On the night of Bush's statement, Body Count performed at the Palace in Los Angeles, on tour with Exodus and sharing a bill with Pantera, White Zombie, and Mighty Joe Young, whose debut would hit stores that September under their new band name, Stone Temple Pilots, after Ernie handed their demo tape to eventual STP manager Steve Stewart. Body Count started their show with a pig-masked man in a police uniform (a fan picked by Ice before the show) getting jumped by Ice, Sean E. Sean, and Sean E. Mac, while the band broke into "Body Count's in the House." Ice slammed Bush and Quayle in "Out in the Parking Lot," before closing with "Cop Killer."

"There were police protests everywhere, and you had to walk past a lot of angry cops," Exodus' Gary Holt remembers the tour. "But [Body Count] were super awesome guys. We shared a lot of laughs," he smiles. "I still have my Rhyme Syndicate jacket that Ice-T gave me."

"I don't know what Bush and Quayle and the rest of these guys are so upset about," Ice told the *LA Times*. "Don't these politicians realize the country was founded on the kind of revolutionary political thought expressed in my song? I mean, haven't they ever listened to the national anthem? Anybody knows that 'The Star-Spangled Banner' is really just a song about a shoot-out between us and the police. Have they forgotten that Paul Revere became a Revolutionary War

.com/culture/2019/11/terminator-dark-fate-border-patrol-villain-t2-lapd .html.

hero for warning everybody, 'The police are coming, the police are coming?'"[28] In *Rolling Stone*, Ice called the Fourth of July "National Fuck the Police Day."[29]

The FBI added Ice-T to the National Threat list, and the IRS audited his taxes twice. His daughter was pulled out of school and asked if her father was involved with any paramilitary organizations. "The minute the president says your name, the most serious background check of your life happens," Ice remembered. "He wants a dossier."[30]

The LAPD, meanwhile, tried rehabilitating its image by hiring their first-ever African American Chief of the LAPD, recruiting Willie L. Williams from Philadelphia. On June 30, the day Williams was sworn in, he condemned "Cop Killer." "I have major problems with it as an American, as a parent, and as a 30-year police officer," stated Williams. "I think it's a disgrace that any singer would use such vulgarity and give the implication that killing an officer is okay."[31]

"People who ride around all night and use crack cocaine and listen to rap music that talks about killing cops—it's

[28]Philips, Chuck. "Cover Story: The Uncivil War: The Battle between the Establishment and Supporters of Rap Music Reopens Old Wounds of Race and Class." *Los Angeles Times*, July 19, 1992.

[29]Light, Alan. "Ice-T: The *Rolling Stone* Interview." *Rolling Stone*, August 20, 1992.

[30]Maron, Marc. "Episode 1145—Ice-T." *WTF with Marc Maron Podcast*, August 3, 2020, http://www.wtfpod.com/podcast/episode-1145-ice-t.

[31]Miles, Jack. "Blacks vs. Browns." *The Atlantic*, October 1, 1992, https://www.theatlantic.com/magazine/archive/1992/10/blacks-vs-browns/306655/.

bound to pump them up," stated Fraternal Order of the Police President Paul Taylor. "No matter what anybody tells you, this kind of music is dangerous."[32]

Numerous defenders of Body Count's First Amendment right to release "Cop Killer" couldn't bring themselves to do so without trashing the song itself, calling the song "repugnant,"[33] "as bad as anything ever put on a record or disc,"[34] or "the cheapest, most conventional image of rebellion that our culture offers."[35] "It was always, 'Well, he has the First Amendment right, I don't agree with him, but . . . ' Fuck that. Back me up on the fact that Ice-T has the grounds to say, 'Fuck the police,' 'cause the police have been killing his people,"[36] Ice stated. For lawmakers, it was easier to attack "Cop Killer" and exploit fears of rap than to reform the issues Body Count were writing about, issues lawmakers themselves had the power to change.

The NRA attempted to occupy the protest, over CLEAT's objections, with their own press conferences and marches,

[32]Chang, Jeff. *Can't Stop Won't Stop: A History of the Hip-Hop Generation.* United States, St. Martin's Press, 2007.

[33]Morris, Chris, et al. "Bush, New LAPD Chief, NRA Assail Body Count; Cops to Sell TW Stock." *Billboard*, July 11, 1992.

[34]Royko, Mike. "Rap Rantings Get Corporate Blessing as Long as They Sell." *Tampa Bay Times*, January 12, 2020, https://www.tampabay.com/archive /1992/06/24/rap-rantings-get-corporate-blessing-as-long-as-they-sell/.

[35]Ehrenreich, Barbara. ". . . Or Is It Creative Freedom?" *Time*, July 20, 1992. http://content.time.com/time/subscriber/article/0,33009,976011,00.html.

[36]Blecha, Peter. *Taboo Tunes: A History of Banned Bands & Censored Songs.* Backbeat Books, 2004.

forcing their own pro-gun stealth PAC Law Enforcement Alliance of America (LEAA) into a Time Warner meeting CLEAT had negotiated. LEAA staged their own news conferences and promised to bring maimed police officers to the shareholders' meeting. NRA Executive VP Wayne LaPierre stated that if Time Warner really cared about reducing violence in America, "They would put an immediate end to distributing this disgusting album."[37] The NRA also placed full-page newspaper ads in numerous papers, "While Time Warner Counts Its Money, America May Count Its Murdered Cops," warning of "a Top 40 album banging the brains of millions of youth, marketed by Time Warner," urging its membership into a letter-writing campaign and threatening legal action.[38]

That week, "Body Count's in the House" appeared as the end credits theme for Sony sci-fi action flick *Universal Soldier*. The conglomerate couldn't risk their multimillion-dollar franchise with an uncensored Body Count song, and the film version carefully edits out the curse words that might have offended the sensibilities of anybody who watched *Universal Soldier*. But in the corresponding music video, which intercuts band performance footage with scenes from the film, Body Count multitracks the vocals, coming on like an army. At the video's conclusion, two police officers

[37]"NRA Joins Police in Saying Song Is out of Line." *Deseret News*, Reuters, June 13, 1992, https://www.deseret.com/1992/6/13/18989108/nra-joins-police-in-saying-song-is-out-of-line-br.

[38]Morris, Chris, et al. "Bush, New LAPD Chief, NRA Assail Body Count; Cops to Sell TW Stock." *Billboard*, July 11, 1992.

confront the band backstage. "You think you're tough, don't you?" one asks. Ice directs the officers to his bodyguards, who step forward to reveal themselves as *Universal Soldier*'s stars, Jean-Claude Van Damme and Dolph Lundgren. Ice smiles while the officers sheepishly retreat.

Watching the band thrash through "Body Count's in the House" amid high-budget action clips, it looks intended as a commercial for Sony Pictures. By the film's July 10 release date, it was a coup for Body Count.

"My experience with Ice-T was very cool," recalls Van Damme. "Fantastic, fantastic."

9
"The tension mounts."

At the July 16 shareholders meeting at the Regent Beverly Wilshire Hotel, Time Warner employees wore Batman lapel pins to celebrate the record-breaking box office success of *Batman Returns*. Booming profits were being reported in publishing, music, film, and TV, including a 4-for-1 stock split and revenue increase to $3.1 billion. While Time Warner CEO Steven J. Ross lay terminally ill with prostate cancer, Gerald Levin stepped up to run the meeting in his absence.

Outside the building, approximately 100 protestors from all over the county, representing at least seventeen different police groups, chanted "Hey hey, ho ho, Time Warner's got to go!," "Burn rap, it's all crap!," and "To hell with Ice-T, he should be smashed!" Among the picket signs were "WHY KILL MY DADDY?", "NO MORE ICE-T FOR ME," and "CALL ICE-T WHEN YOU NEED HELP! NOT!," including some repeat messages. Other signs included the names of slain police officers. Ron DeLord held a sign listing Time Warner products to boycott, and Glenn White pulled up in a Dallas police car.

Ice was with Ortiz and Little Ice in his Rolls Royce when their car stopped on the corner of Beverly and Wilshire. "We were going to sign the mortgage and paperwork for our home," says Ortiz. "Before you know it, we were waiting at a red light, and we saw these people. He said, 'You've got to effing be kidding me.'"

"One of them told the others, you could see it unfolding. 'That's him. That's him.' They were saying some really awful things, and he just rolled the window down, stuck his hand out and gave them the finger. By the time we finished filling out that paperwork and made it home, that picture was in the news."

The protestors found a one-hour photo shop and had the picture developed in time to bring it to the shareholders' meeting. "It gave us a lot of satisfaction that we were finally getting to him," White recalled.[1]

Inside the building, a Xeroxed copy of Phyllis Pollack's *Billboard* editorial "Uninformed Media Serve Ice-T Bashers' Aims" was distributed to prepare attendees. Shareholders were invited to make comments before the agenda items, one of which was "Cop Killer." Hinojosa watched NRA reps attempt to coach one surly, elderly minor shareholder.

The shareholder rose, exhibiting the chiseled features and commanding voice that had made Charlton Heston one of Hollywood's most admired leading men. Heston scolded Ice, "who's trying for his fifteen minutes of fame," while admonishing "the responsible officials in this company" for releasing the record. He brought up the promotional body bags the label

[1]Moll, George. "Behind the Music: Ice-T." Season 4, episode 4, VH1, August 27, 2000.

had sent out. ("Isn't that cute?") And Charlton Heston read the lyrics to "Cop Killer" out loud for the shocked attendees.

Heston recalled the event in his autobiography. "'Mr. Levin,' I said. 'Jews and homosexuals are also sometimes attacked, though of course not as often as police officers. Let me ask you: If this piece were titled, 'Fag Killer,' or if the lyrics went, 'Die, die, die, kike, die!' would you still peddle it? It's often been said that if Adolf Hitler came back with a dynamite treatment for a film, every studio in town would be after it. Would Warner be among them?'"[2] Heston capped his performance by reading the lyrics to "KKK Bitch" and asking shareholders to censure the board.

"Here I was with Ben-Hur and Moses, all rolled into one," remembered 2 Live Crew prosecuting attorney Jack Thompson, sent to represent Oliver North's Freedom Alliance at the meeting. "And when Heston stood up, it was really a reprise of Moses confronting Pharaoh."[3]

"To have him recite lyrics is on par with William Shatner reciting Bob Dylan," says Merlis. "It just comes off silly. But he made his point."

DeLord spoke after Heston. "If you target people for killing and say it over and over again, what makes you different from [Nazi propagandist Joseph] Goebbels?"[4]

---

[2]Heston, Charlton. *In the Arena: An Autobiography*. United States, Boulevard Books, 1997.

[3]"HipHop PT2—e." *YouTube*, November 27, 2010, https://youtu.be /04aFZ52pRR4.

[4]Hall, Carla. "Charlton Heston's Rap Against Ice-T: Actor, Others Protest Lyrics at Time Warner Meeting." *The Washington Post*, July 17, 1992.

"Ice-T is simply a criminal sociopath who can rhyme. Time Warner is knowingly training people, especially young people, to kill," stated Thompson.[5]

The ballroom of 1,000 was silent as police officers who had been blinded in the line of duty spoke. "I don't have a normal relationship with my two and a half-year-old son because I can't catch the ball and throw it back," said Louisiana training officer Bobby Smith, "because someone hated the police so bad that they took away my sight for no reason at all."[6]

DeLord watched Beverly Sills, a former opera star and Time Warner board member who'd been crusading for the company to drop Ice-T, cry while the officers spoke. "I knew then we had won," he recalls. "They just didn't put a human face on the police side of this argument. Whether police officers should or shouldn't have dealt with someone in a certain way is not the issue. There's 800,000 police officers out there, and we can't advocate killing them as some solution to social injustice."

"You can be for social justice, you can be that police have mishandled cases, or you can accuse them of racism, or systemic racism in our own criminal justice system," says DeLord. "The point was, you can't be a corporation, particularly in the family entertainment business, who allows someone to target anyone . . . for violence or death."

[5]Thompson, Jack. *Out of Harm's Way*. United States, Tyndale House Publishers, 2006.

[6]Reckard, E. Scott. "Police Square Off Against Time Warner in 'Cop Killer' Dispute." Associated Press, July 15, 1992, https://apnews.com/article/015 01439dd13434ddaa330eef86cc409.

Time Warner spokesman Ed Adler insisted the promotional body bags referred to "an anti-drug song which talked about kids coming home in body bags. It was in no way a reference to cops in body bags."[7] But Levin took most of the heat. "What would it profit anyone if, in the name of pleasing everyone, the country's leading media and entertainment company ceased to risk saying anything worth listening to?" he asked. "We must help ensure that the voices of the powerless, the disenfranchised, those at the margins are heard." He added, "We have nothing but the deepest respect and admiration of the men and women of America's law enforcement agencies."[8] By the end of the five-hour meeting, Levin had proposed continuing the discourse with a commercial-free TV program that invited police, artists, and citizens to participate in community-building.

"Charlton Heston is somebody who they could bring out and use in this issue, and people somehow because he was in a movie, believe he's Moses," Ice stated. "He also is a member of the NRA, who lobbies to keep a bullet called the 'cop killer' legal, the one that's a Teflon nine bullet that can rip through a police bulletproof vest. That should be legal? I don't know why."[9] Ice was correct that the NRA had lobbied

[7]Hall, Carla. "Charlton Heston's Rap Against Ice-T: Actor, Others Protest Lyrics at Time Warner Meeting." *The Washington Post*, July 17, 1992.

[8]Dexter, Pete. "Charlton Heston Gets to the Heart of the Hypocrisy in Hollywood." *Deseret News*, July 26, 1992, https://www.deseret.com/1992/7/26/18996340/charlton-heston-gets-to-the-heart-of-the-hypocrisy-in-hollywood.

[9]"Ice-T Rockumentary." *YouTube*, July 28, 2019, https://youtu.be/gD2Q-Rg8zyY.

against the ban of "cop killer" Teflon bullets. During the Body Count controversy, the NRA were spending millions to halt the anti-gun violence Brady Bill in Congress, against the endorsement of nearly every major American police organization, working to put more police lives at risk than all the rappers in the world combined.

"Mo, who is a real civil libertarian, he and Lenny fought very, very hard to protect Ice, he called me into his office and said 'Howie, there's nothing more we can do. The pressure from Time Warner is so heavy that, we fought this for months, and we can't anymore. If you want to go and fight with them, you have my blessing.'" Says Klein. He was flown to the New York offices to meet with corporate. "They only had one concern, which was the share price."

"We sat around for at least at least two hours fighting about it. . . . There were six of them, but there were three who were sort of leading the pack. People in charge of finances, they were all way above, there was no one from the Warner Music Group, it was all corporate. And at one point, they just basically said, 'Fuck you and fuck you.' And they got up, all six of them rose at once and they walked out of the room," says Klein. "They don't care what I think or what I have to say, Ice-T has to be dropped. And if I didn't like it, I could quit or they could fire me."

"I love the songs, every single one of them. I love all the guys in the band," says Klein. "I love that song and didn't want to see it removed."

"It's one thing to say, 'no one's gonna buy this record,'" says Stewart. "When you start to say, 'Hey, we're gonna have your institutional investors take your money out of your company," that became very scary to them."

Ice remembered a Warner Music conversation in a *Vibe* interview with Chuck D. "Mo Ostin and I were sitting at a 20-seat boardroom table. He said, 'Ice, you're a part of Time Warner's record division. Let me explain the record division.' He took a quarter out of his pocket, flipped it onto the table and said, 'This table is Time Warner. That quarter is the record division.' In other words, he was saying, I'm the boss of this quarter, but look how big the company is."

"Ice took it as far as anybody could take it," said Chuck D. "That motherfucker had the Fraternal Order of Police and the president actually making comments."

"Isn't that some kind of juice?" asked *Vibe*.

"The kind that will get you killed." Ice responded.[10]

Billboard reported a July 18 Las Vegas incident in which two patrol officers were fired on and five Black teens were arrested, with one teen possibly singing "Cop Killer" lyrics. "We don't know for sure. The officers did hear one or two of the youths mumble some of the lyrics from that song," stated Las Vegas Police Deputy Chief John Sullivan.[11] Ice addressed the story on *Arsenio*. "He already had determined

[10]Smith, Danyel. "Juice: Who's Got the Power?" *Vibe*, September 1996.
[11]Harrington, Richard. "On the Beat: Time for a Crackdown?" *The Washington Post*, July 29, 1992.

that he wanted to kill cops. Anybody who listens to a record or watches TV or anything and goes out and acts is unstable from the beginning."[12] The *Arsenio* show received threatening calls and were told they could no longer count on police responses leading up to Ice's July 21 appearance, which included a pulverizing Body Count performance of "There Goes the Neighborhood." "He was taking a big chance by putting us on there, because everyone else was dropping us," says Ernie. "He was a little tense."

Corporations including Chrysler and General Motors canceled advertising campaigns in Time Warner publications such as *Time*, *Entertainment Weekly*, and *People*, costing an estimated $150 million.[13] Police organizations in New York, Boston, Philadelphia, and more petitioned their pension fund boards to divest their stakes in Time Warner. Police pressured city council to block Time Warner's local cable franchises in cities like Houston and Indianapolis. "There was so much going on that we didn't keep track of it," says Ernie. "All that we did was just play the song every night. We never have stopped playing the song."

Time Warner released an interview clip to the press of Ice-T telling people to not kill cops. But Ice's penchant for code-switching started being scrutinized and used against

[12]"Ice-T on Arsenio Hall Show 1992." *YouTube*, February 21, 2020, https://youtu.be/muACyshkNos.

[13]Kot, Greg. "Unsilenced by Right Wing, Ice-T Takes His Messages to New Label." *News & Record*, April 10, 1993, https://greensboro.com/unsilenced-by-right-wing-ice-t-takes-his-messages-to-new-label/article_b3457c3e-46f7-5546-8ca1-3b9653364ba6.html.

him. On July 23, NBC's *Today Show* broadcasted clips from a camcorder video of Ice outside of KJLH on May 1, talking to an LA crowd on day three of the uprising, cursing out and venting for the destruction police stations and the White House. That night on PBS, *MacNeil/Lehrer NewsHour* co-host Jim Lehrer introduced the show's lead story: "A piece of rap music called 'Cop Killer.'" Def Jam President David Harleston was on hand to debate DeLord, but learned at the taping a new opponent would be video broadcasted in.

Charlton Heston promised to read Ice's comments from the *Today Show* video. "I'm going to bleep this," Heston stated. "Use your imagination. 'The police ain't 'bleep' to me. They never will be. They're a gestapo organization, till you start takin' them cops down out there in the street, then you all are really still 'bleeping' in the wind. . . . But niggers ain't ready to smoke no pig. I personally would like to blow some 'bleeping' police stations up. If it was up to me, I would burn the White House down.'"

Heston also claimed that the original album cover "showed Ice-T standing with a gun over a prostrate police officer" and that Time Warner had previously "insisted on changing the original title of the whole album, which was *Cop Killer*, to *Body Bag*."

"There is, in my mind, no more likelihood that a music listener of the song 'Cop Killer' is going to go out and kill a cop than there is the likelihood that singing 'The Battle Hymn of the Republic' is going to lead to international war." Harleston stated. "Ice-T is conveying to this country, whether we want to hear it or not, that we are in trouble, our cities are in trouble, our citizens are in trouble. Anybody who has been subject to something like police brutality, brutality brought about on account of the victim's race knows about that anger. And for those of us who have not been subject to it, we need to know about it."[14]

One can watch Ice's rant, with more context, on YouTube. "For ten years, myself, people like Ice Cube, Public Enemy, have predicted this situation. And we've been shut off by the radio stations and the media, as being just Black kids yelling. We yelled about police brutality. We yelled about the gang situation. Me, myself personally, I'm just unhappy with the focus of the anger," Ice says before the clips aired. He calls out America's invasions of Panama and the Persian Gulf, knocks President Bush for sowing racial divisions, and concludes, "If the Blacks and Hispanics and Asians and white people get together, the people that are really down with us, they can't fuck with us, we provin' that right now."[15]

On Friday, July 24, the day after the *Today* clips aired, Body Count played a sold-out show at North Hollywood's Electric Ballroom. *Billboard* and *Variety* reported between 60 and 100 police officers and surrounding the venue by car, helicopter, motorcycle, on foot, and on rooftop, including fire marshals, FBI agents in an unmarked vehicle, and City Councilman Joel Wachs. Event organizers installed

[14]*The MacNeil/Lehrer Newshour*. American Archive of Public Broadcasting, https://americanarchive.org/catalog/cpb-aacip_507-np1wd3qt9w.

[15]"2Pac Ice T—Poverty Violence Racism Black White Hispanic People Together." *YouTube*, January 6, 2012, https://youtu.be/7f9hyhVnkZk.

metal detectors. Protest groups held up signs outside and were received "by a horde of media worthy of a sports championship," including at least eight news trucks.[16] Attendees included a recent release from Los Angeles' Men's Central Jail ("Everybody down there is talking about Ice-T.") and a couple visiting from Tokyo ("Killing cops is bad, but I just love the music. I just love the way people in America get so excited about these things.").[17] No arrests were reported.

"They brought the SWAT team out. They brought cops on horses and things like that. But there was no problem with us. In our show, they were peaceful and they went on like they should. It was just the cops creating this controversy," says Ernie.

None of the crowd could have known that earlier that day, Ice and Hinojosa met with Ostin, Waronker, Klein, Merlis, and Stein in the Burbank office. They agreed to not inform Warner's corporate executives of the decision until the press conference four days later, giving Ice time to back out of it if he chose. Insiders remember shock and sadness at the table when Ice stated his decision to take the song off the record. But nobody tried to change his mind.

[16]Augusto, Troy J. "Body Count." *Variety*, July 28, 1992, https://variety.com/1992/legit/reviews/body-count-1200430252/.

[17]Kaplan, Tracey and Jim Zamora. "The Heat Turns out for Ice-T Rap Concert." *Los Angeles Times*, July 25, 1992.

10
"Just watch what you say."

Klein was in his office packing a framed gold *Body Count* record for shipment when Waronker stopped by. Waronker read the award's plaque: PRESENTED TO VICE PRESIDENT DAN QUAYLE. Another award had been printed for Charlton Heston. "He said, 'Can you just please wait till after the election?,'" says Klein. "I wound up basically using it to raise money for a civil liberties group."

"This was Ice-T's solution," says Merlis. "He said, 'I don't want to put you guys in a bad situation. We'll take the song off.'"

"Ice just called and said 'We're gonna pull that song.' I'm like 'OK, cool.' That's the way our conversations generally are, he just runs it by me, and the decisions are good," says Ernie. "We made our point. We said the song. The song is always there."

"People were getting threatened that we liked and that we cared for. . . . It was our fight, our song, it was written by us in that room. It wasn't really their fight."

On the night CLEAT ended their boycott, Warner Bros. Clint Eastwood film *Unforgiven* premiered in Los Angeles, recounting the story of a cop killer avenging a Black man murdered by a corrupt sheriff. It would go on to win the Best Picture Oscar, in a year that also saw violence against bad cops in hit films *Basic Instinct*, *Unlawful Entry*, and *Bad Lieutenant*, and even a major plot point around "cop killer bullets" in Warner's *Lethal Weapon 3*, 1992's second-highest grossing film.

"It's easy to pass judgment when you don't know what the fuck's going on," Ice stated. "Because in a war—and make no mistake, this is a war—sometimes you have to retreat and return with superior firepower."[1]

Ice graced the August 20, 1992, cover of *Rolling Stone* in a full policeman's uniform, complete with a billy club, "Ice-T" nameplate, badge, and combination cap. The story filled out the next issue's entire letters to the editor page with responses. The Mark Seliger photo is now one of the magazine's most iconic covers, a more combative image of Ice-T than a picture of him flashing gang signs or giving the finger would have been. "They're yelling about a record that came out in March, and just yesterday the cops were killing people out in the street," Ice quipped in the profile. "Why all this protest about a record that speaks about killing cops and not protest against the cops killing kids out there in the streets?"[2]

"They're saying: 'Hold up, these rappers are talking to me, and it's making me understand. Why did John Wayne always

[1]Ice-T, and Heidi Siegmund Cuda. *The Ice Opinion: Who Gives a Fuck?* St. Martin's Press, 1994.

[2]Light, Alan. "Ice-T: The *Rolling Stone* Interview." *Rolling Stone* August 20, 1992.

win? Weren't we taking that land from the Indians? Haven't we been kind of fucked-up to people?' They're starting to figure it out," Ice told the magazine.[3]

Ice offered "Cop Killer" to Jello Biafra's Alternative Tentacles label but ended up printing 10,000 copies of the record himself and gave them away at concerts. Meanwhile, Ernie returned to Lollapalooza to perform "Cop Killer" on stage in Miami, this time with Soundgarden. "Chris [Cornell] says, 'Ernie, we're covering one of your songs,'" Ernie remembers. "They restrung the guitar so I could play it left-handed."

Warner sent retailers a letter detailing return instructions, with all expenses prepaid. Store owners ignored the request and watched the collector's item, first-edition record fly off shelves. Resellers across the country, in some cases, ordered hundreds of copies.[4] Magic Disk in Compton raised the album price and still sold out. Warner also couldn't make stores stock the new version, and sales of the *Body Count* reissue sagged. Who'd prefer a censored record?

Speaking with *A Current Affair*'s Jana Wendt, Ice fielded a question about critics saying Body Count's music took a backseat to the controversial lyrics. "That's like me saying Rembrandt would have never sold a painting if he didn't paint nudes."[5]

The music industry's most powerful players were expected to comment, from Madonna in *NME* ("I don't know the real

[3]Light, Alan. "Rappers Sounded Warning." *Rolling Stone*, July 9, 1992.

[4]*Newsweek* staff. "The Iceman Concedeth." *Newsweek*, August 9, 1992, https://www.newsweek.com/iceman-concedeth-198038.

[5]"Ice-T (Bodycount) A Current Affair Interview 1992." *YouTube*, January 3, 2012, https://youtu.be/uYLrvAs9_9c.

reason he took it off. Some said he took it off because there were all these people at Time Warner who were getting death threats and people really felt their lives were in danger. Other people say he took it off the record to prove he didn't have it on there to make money. I mean, whoever really knows these things?")[6] to Neil Young in *Musician* ("Ice is great so wherever he goes it's gonna be great. . . . I think what he did with 'Cop Killer' indicates that people don't understand art. They think art is obvious.").[7] David Geffen compared distribution of *Body Count* to selling cocaine.[8] That September, Ernie received a phone call from Duff McKagan. "He calls me up and says, 'Ernie, what's your band doing. . . . Can you be at Arrowhead Stadium in like two days?'"

Faith No More were dropping off their opening spot on the era's biggest metal tour, Guns N' Roses and Metallica's co-headlining stadium jaunt. Body Count were getting in cahoots with the bands, with McKagan hyping them on MTV ("Body Count! I love Body Count.")[9] and Axl Rose wearing a Body Count hat in GNR's "Garden of Eden" video. That fall,

[6]Martin, Gavin. "Madonna: Dominatrix of the Trade." *New Musical Express*, Oct 3, 1992, https://www.rocksbackpages.com/library/article/madonna-dominatrix-of-the-trade.

[7]Rowland, Mark. "The Men on the Harvest Moon: Young-Buck!" *Musician*, Apr. 1993, https://www.rocksbackpages.com/library/article/the-men-on-the-harvest-moon-young-buck.

[8]AP. "Taking The Rap For Rap -- Record Companies Suffer Backlash About Rowdy Musical Lyrics." *The Seattle Times*, July 23, 1992, https://archive.seattletimes.com/archive/?date=19920723&slug=1503591.

[9]"Ice-T • Body Count Interview • Featuring Duff from Guns N' Roses • 1992." *YouTube*, July 24, 2017, https://youtu.be/fSDEYz5ej48.

Ice presented the "Best Rap Video" award at the MTV VMAs 1992 with Metallica's Lars Ulrich and Kirk Hammett, making "Cop Killer" and "family values" jokes from the stage.[10] Ulrich would name *Body Count* in his year's top five records for *Rolling Stone*, stating, "Controversy or not, I think Ice-T isn't capable of doing anything bad."[11]

"They had more broken equipment than we had equipment that works," Ernie recalled the tour.[12] "It felt like an ant on the stage with elephants. . . . That's what I learned from that, how big rock 'n' roll can be."

"We rocked that shit," says Ice. "We got to see Axl Rose throw the mic in the audience every night, all the tour buses and helicopters, that's when you're rolling with the big boys . . . it was a great experience."

"They're just good people," says Ernie. "Axl, one time, they were on stage getting ready to play something. He says, 'Hold on.' He made Slash go get another guitar. And he played 'Out ta Get Me' for Body Count."

But Governor Pete Wilson insisted that Body Count be dropped from the California bill, and the band was removed from two stadium shows by concert promoter Brian Murphy, who called Body Count "inappropriate." Rose lashed out at

[10]"Lars & Kirk from Metallica (and Ice T) Present the 'Best Rap Video' Award at the '92 MTV VMAS." *YouTube*, July 31, 2021, https://youtu.be/nJISfsHpMkk.

[11]"Artists' Picks." *Rolling Stone*, March 4, 1993.

[12]Coyle, Doc. "Ernie C (Body Count)." *The Ex-Man with Doc Coyle*, April 27, 2020, https://www.soundtalentmedia.com/show/the-ex-man-with-doc-coyle/ernie-c-body-count/.

the decision, stating, "Freedom of speech is OK, as long as it doesn't piss off some public official."[13] San Diego mayor Maureen O'Conner was pushed to address Body Count's scheduled appearance on the bill at the city's Jack Murphy Stadium, stating through a press secretary, "The mayor doesn't like the song, but she also feels the city has no place in determining the content of a concert."[14]

One week before the performance, San Diego Police Officers Association president Harry O. Eastus II sent a letter to the show's promoters and the press demanding that Body Count be removed from the bill, calling the performance "a real slap in the face." Earlier that summer, Eastus had publicly pressured Mayor O'Connor into dropping 24-hour-a-day police protection, after the mayor had refused to join six other council members in condemning "Cop Killer."[15]

Citing concerns about police refusing to work the show, Murphy Stadium director Bill Wilson, a former Pasadena police officer, sent a letter urging promoters to consider two options: "1) Replace the band" or "2) Have the band not play the song 'Cop Killer.'" A record number of police (233) and security officers (1,200) were called in for the stadium's biggest show in years, reportedly "double the number of

[13]Hochman, Steve. "Ice-T Is 'Vetoed' from 2 Guns Shows." *Los Angeles Times*, September 24, 1992.

[14]Lee, John H. "Attempt to Bar Ice-T from Stadium Fails: Entertainment: City Officials and Police Group Determine That No Grounds Exist to Stop Concert." *Los Angeles Times*, September 25, 1992.

[15]Platte, Mark. "Mayor Gives up Police Guards after Criticism." *Los Angeles Times*, August 27, 1992.

security personnel ever hired for a stadium event." But after negotiations, promoters released a statement that the show was under control, with one representative calling Ice-T "very considerate of the security concerns, and he is not out to cause problems for anyone, police included."[16] Body Count would remain on the bill. "It's my understanding that he has agreed not to play 'Cop Killer,'" Brian Murphy assured officials.[17]

Body Count wrapped up "Momma's Gotta Die Tonight" near the hour mark of their set, when Ice walked to center stage and produced a note. He read the Eastus letter out loud for thousands of fans, while officers rushed through the stadium's tunnels toward the stage. Ice stuffed the letter down the front of his pants. The band tore into "Cop Killer."

"This shows everyone what a butt he is," Eastus told the press.[18]

Body Count continued to be antagonized by cops. *Entertainment Weekly* reported a Fort Lauderdale former police officer printing and selling T-shirts depicting Ice-T targeted in crosshairs: "Let's 'Ice' T."[19] Local police

[16]Lee, John H. "Attempt to Bar Ice-T from Stadium Fails: Entertainment: City Officials and Police Group Determine That No Grounds Exist to Stop Concert." *Los Angeles Times*, September 25, 1992.

[17]"1992.09.30—Jack Murphy Stadium, San Diego, USA." *Appetite for Discussion*, https://www.a-4-d.com/t1961-1992-09-30-jack-murphy -stadium-san-diego-usa.

[18]Granberry, Michael. "Ice-T Violates Pledge by Promoters, Sings 'Cop Killer' on Stage." *Los Angeles Times*, October 1, 1992.

[19]Bruno, Karen. "A Controversial Ice-T Shirt." *Entertainment Weekly*, September 18, 1992, https://ew.com/article/1992/09/18/controversial-ice-t -shirt/.

organizations demanded that concert promoters cancel Ice-T's appearances, and officers refused to provide security for Body Count shows. An Ice-T show at the Metropol in Pittsburgh that December was canceled when local police officers refused to work,[20] with an ACLU investigation finding "police officers also threatened to delay response times and otherwise be less cooperative and less effective in addressing the club's needs if the show were to proceed."[21] A Fraternal Order of the Police lodge tried to stop a Maryland Ice-T performance with Public Enemy, stating that Ice's music "tarnishes the minds of youth."[22] *Rolling Stone* reported Body Count and Ice facing "resistance from local police in cities such as Boston, Philadelphia and Poughkeepsie."[23]

On tour, Body Count parked as close as they could to each venue to avoid protestors. At the Vic Theatre in Chicago that December, protestors mobbed Body Count's bus and threw disposables at the band. "They were all around the building," says Ortiz, who remembers carrying her one-year-old son past the protestors. "I'm holding him and some stuff starts

[20]"Ice-T Concert Canceled Because Pittsburgh Police Won't Work at Show." UPI, December 16, 1992, https://www.upi.com/Archives/1992/12/16/Ice-T-concert-canceled-because-Pittsburgh-police-wont-work-at-show/3809724482000/.

[21]Light, Alan. "Body Count Shows Canceled." *Rolling Stone*, February 4, 1993.

[22]Harrington, Richard. "On the Beat: Police Rap Ice-T's Md. Concert." *The Washington Post*, November 18, 1992.

[23]Light, Alan. "Body Count Shows Canceled." *Rolling Stone*, February 4, 1993.

getting tossed. . . . I was nervous because I had the baby. And I just remember handing him to Mooseman, him saying 'Give him to me,' and he literally took him and put him under his coat, and we were running in."

A reported 400 off-duty officers in civilian clothes were outside the Vic with a SWAT team, carrying signs with the names of slain police officers, singing "The Star-Spangled Banner" and chanting, "No more Ice-T, CPD" (Chicago Police Department).[24] "You'd get to the stadiums and clubs, and they'd have families and people out there with signs, yelling out all this horrible stuff to us," says Ortiz. "That was almost that whole year."

"They followed us through Christmas," Ice stated in a Body Count interview from Hawaii. "What do you call a cop picketing outside a Body Count concert in the middle of December in Chicago? A 'copsicle.' That's what you get, stupid motherfuckers."[25]

While on tour with Body Count, Ice received a call that Time Warner execs above Ostin had deemed the upcoming *Home Invasion* cover art unacceptable. The record was reviewed by the same Warner "crisis attorney" who reviewed Martin Scorsese's *The Last Temptation of Christ* and postponed to 1993 to minimize controversy. Ice's soundtrack hit "Ricochet,"

---

[24]Hill, Mary. "Off-Duty Officers Wear Badges of Protest for Ice-T Concert." *Chicago Tribune*, December 29, 1992, https://www.chicagotribune.com/news/ct-xpm-1992-12-29-9204280329-story.html.

[25]"Ice T and Body Count 1992 Hawaii Rare Concert Footage." *YouTube*, April 29, 2011, https://youtu.be/XseyD-ipJ9U.

including lyrics about cop's blood on his sneakers, was moved to a bonus disc titled *The Last Temptation of Ice.*

Unlike previous protests, the *Home Invasion* controversy was coming from the top of the conglomerate itself, with the corporation suppressing Ice's ideas before they could be released. "It wasn't clear where that was coming from," says Stewart. "We'd had seemingly the full support of the top of the company, but that changed somewhere in there."

"The corporation was very ill at ease and our chairman Mo Ostin, who had high regard for Ice-T, as an artist and as an artistic thinker, made an offer to Ice-T that he would release him from his contract, which was a painful thing to do," says Merlis. "Mo Ostin was very, very resolute in saying, 'Well, artistic freedom is the bulwark of what we do.' But ultimately the corporation said you got to do something about this."

In January 1993, Hinojosa asked for Ice-T and Body Count to be released from their contracts. Days later, they met with Warner execs to work out a deal that released Ice and let him keep the *Home Invasion* master tapes. Majors shied away from him, but Ice was able to sign with independent Priority Records. "Warner Bros. cannot afford to be in the business of Black rage," Ice stated.[26]

"He did the pre-emptive strike because he's a player like that. He's going to shape his own narrative. But I'm sure they would have shit-canned him, because they could not take the heat," says Cuda.

---

[26]Ice-T, and Heidi Siegmund Cuda. *The Ice Opinion: Who Gives a Fuck?* United States, St. Martin's Press, 1994.

"It destroyed Warner Bros.' reputation in a lot of ways, especially with Black artists," says Klein. "It took decades for that to be repaired."

"Ice-T was a terrific artist who spoke the truth," stated Ostin. "But the corporation got so thin-skinned after the incident at the shareholders' meeting. In the end, Ice-T decided to leave because he could not allow tampering with his work. And I can't blame him."[27]

The issue stayed a political football, with Senate Majority Leader Bob Dole, weeks after announcing his 1996 presidential run, stating, "Ice-T of 'Cop Killer' fame is one of Time Warner's 'stars.' I cannot bring myself to repeat the lyrics of some of the 'music' Time Warner promotes. But our children do."[28]

"You've got two options: You can become very cynical or you can have some kind of hope. And I've got hope. I don't think it's necessarily gonna change in my lifetime," Ice stated. "Especially racial issues. 'Cause you've got 400 years of one situation, and people who are locked into these traditional modes."

"So I have to look forward. Hope is all I have."[29]

[27]Hilburn, Robert, and Chuck Philips. "Cover Story: Quotations from Chairman Mo: Mo Ostin Let His Artists Do the Talking for Him His Whole Career. Now the Record-Biz Legend Steps out of the Shadows and Takes Us on a Tour from Ol' Blue Eyes to Red Hot Chili Peppers." *Los Angeles Times*, December 11, 1994.

[28]Dole, Robert. "Remarks in Los Angeles: 'Hollywood Speech.'" American Presidency Project, May 31, 1995, https://www.presidency.ucsb.edu/documents/remarks-los-angeles-hollywood-speech.

[29]Rowland, Mark. "Ice-T: Crap Killer." *Musician*, Jan. 1993, https://www.rocksbackpages.com/library/article/ice-t-crap-killer.

First *Home Invasion* single "I Ain't New Ta This" showed Ice in top form, though he told *Vox* magazine he was excited about a different song. "This year, the girls are going to be hot on me because of '99 Problems.'"[30] In *The Ice Opinion*, he gauged the song's hit potential and his inability to compromise. "Change the word 'bitch' to girl and it's a pop record, not a street record," he noted. "I can sell that one to Vanilla Ice."[31]

Home Invasion was released in March. It debuted while the number one song in America was "Informer," by Warner Music white reggae-rapper Snow, which topped the *Billboard* Hot 100 for seven weeks and inspired a Jim Carrey parody on *In Living Color*, titled "Imposter:" "Time Warner kicked Ice-T off the label for dissing the cops, they said it just ain't right / But when a Caucasian man records a cop-hating song, they don't have a problem, must be an oversight."[32]

Plans for *Ice-T's Players*, *Ice-TV*, and a *New Jack City* sequel were all scrapped. The synergy deal was off the table. OGG didn't make it to retailers.[33] *Looters* was renamed *Trespass*, given a less violent ending and postponed until Christmas to avoid association with the LA uprising. Dutton, Hyperion, and Simon & Schuster were among the publishers who expressed

[30]Iley, Chrissy. "I've Robbed Enough Houses to See What People Have." *Vox*, February 1, 1993.

[31]Ice-T, and Heidi Siegmund Cuda. *The Ice Opinion: Who Gives a Fuck?* United States, St. Martin's Press, 1994.

[32]"Imposter (Snow) - Jim Carrey." *YouTube*, April 13, 2006, https://youtu.be /Icb_tRTnA4g.

[33]Harrington, Richard. "The Ice-T Progression: From Musical Gangsta to TV Cop." *The Washington Post*, March 2, 2003.

and then withdrew interest in Ice's book. *The Ice Opinion: Who Gives a Fuck?* was eventually published by St. Martin's Press in 1994. Remnants of *Ice-TV* can be seen in Ice's enjoyable 1994 TV special *Kiss My Baadasss: Ice-T's Guide to Blaxploitation.*[34]

Despite being an artist who wears age and experience well—he ain't new ta this—Ice was pushing forty in an ageist game that, pre-artists like Jay-Z, didn't have long careers after thirty. *Home Invasion* was Ice's last gold record, and his audience decreased over the late nineties. He moved more of his hustle to acting, metal, and releasing music online before it hit stores. He ran the digital record label Coroner Records ("The old-school major labels are going to die, only the coroner will continue to have a job."[35]) and opened an office on Hollywood Boulevard. "Anybody who's ever seen it actually work cannot honestly believe CDs got a chance in hell in the next five-10 years," Ice explained MP3s and CD-ripping in a 1999 home studio interview.[36]

Ice appeared in an estimated thirty-seven films from 1997 to 2014, nearly all straight to video. But roles in a couple of Dick Wolf projects led to a call for *Law & Order: Special*

[34]"Ice-T Presents Kiss My Baadasssss (1994)." YouTube, December 5, 2018, https://youtu.be/ZpllSg2AiQ4.

[35]Zwerin, Mike, and International Herald Tribune. "Beyond 'Cop Killer': Ice T and the 7th Deadly Sin." *The New York Times*, September 22, 1999, https://www.nytimes.com/1999/09/22/style/IHT-beyond-cop-killerice-t-and-the-7th-deadly-sin.html.

[36]Neilstein, Vince. "Video: Ice T Predicted the Decline of the Music Industry in 1999." *MetalSucks*, March 20, 2017, https://www.metalsucks.net/2017/03/20/video-ice-t-predicted-the-decline-of-the-music-industry-in-1999/.

Victims Unit in 2000. At the time, Ice was thinking more about Coroner Records, but he went to New York to film four episodes. He is now the longest-running Black actor in TV history.

"Your grandmothers know him," said Ernie. "People see our videos and the comments are like, 'Isn't that the guy from *Law & Order?*'"[37]

It's a role that baffles some of the same people who thought Ice-T wasn't smart enough to be creating characters in his Body Count lyrics, and can't believe he'd create another one for TV. But playing a policeman got more people talking about Ice-T and brought more people to his music. He's more recognized today as the hardboiled, one-liner-spouting Odafin "Fin" Tutuola than the man who terrorized conservative America, adored as Fin by people who might have detained him for being Ice. "Cops are now some of my biggest fans," Ice reflected.[38]

[37]Turman, Katherine. "Body Count: 'Cop Killer' to Manslaughter." *The Village Voice*, May 11, 2017, https://www.villagevoice.com/2014/06/11/body-count-cop-killer-to-manslaughter/.

[38]Ice-T and Douglas Century. *Ice: A Memoir of Gangster Life and Redemption-from South Central to Hollywood*. United States, Random House Publishing Group, 2011.

11
"You'll be six feet underground."

By September 1993, rap and metal were close enough for the *Judgment Night* soundtrack, featuring eleven collaborations between rock and rap artists. Ice teamed up with Slayer (Kerry King: "I thought if we're gonna do it with anybody that's not in the heavy metal genre, Ice-T's the guy.")[1] to whip a three-song Exploited medley into "Disorder," which has been a fierce staple of Body Count live shows ever since.

Like many Black artists and metal acts, Body Count were often more appreciated overseas, enough to sign with Virgin and spend much of 1993 playing sold-out shows to European fans, although a show in Italy ended early when Italian punks started gobbing on the band. Ice clocked one of them with the mic stand, a riot broke out and the band left mid-encore. "The fans saw that, they went crazy," says Sean E. Sean. "It felt like *The Warriors*."

[1]"Slayer & Ice-T—Interview & Studio Report 1993." *YouTube*, July 6, 2019, https://youtu.be/dVzLdbNVFFA.

"They told me in Italy 'Oh, we have a custom in Italy— when we like you, we spit on you,'" Ice remembered. "I'm like, 'We got a custom in LA—when you spit on us, we hit you in the head with hard objects.'"[2]

Body Count stayed major metal figures in the early 1990s, with Ernie producing fractured Black Sabbath's nadir-era *Forbidden*, featuring an Ice appearance, and Ice joining Motörhead with Ugly Kid Joe's Whitfield Crane for "Born to Raise Hell," a single and music video for the metal comedy *Airheads*. Body Count resurfaced with another first-person shooter song, rendering a faithful "Hey Joe" for 1993's *Stone Free: A Tribute to Jimi Hendrix*. The CD single featured the same gun illustration from Body Count's record sleeve, equating Body Count's feared violence with a classic, traditional murder ballad by a beloved hard rock artist.

"Hey Joe" also appeared on *Born Dead*, Body Count's more somber sophomore album, released September 1994 with a morbid Halili-illustrated cover. D-Roc and Mooseman stepped up into songwriting, with Moose's "Necessary Evil" getting a music video and "Drive By" becoming one of Body Count's most-performed songs. The closing track, the predominately spoken word "Born Dead," takes things up a notch and was performed with "Necessary Evil" on MTV's *Jon Stewart Show*. ("He was young and goofy and fun," says Ernie.) But *Born Dead* fell off the charts swiftly, and critics were happy to use the album's title as a description in their reviews.

[2]Tannenbaum, Rob. "Ice-T: Sold on Ice." *GQ*, March 1994, https://www.rocksbackpages.com/library/article/ice-t-sold-on-ice.

"It was such a weird zone, because now people are so concerned with what you're going to say," remembers Ice. "Like, 'Oh, these guys are gonna go break the rules again.' I wasn't really doing it for shock value. I'm writing the songs that mattered to me at the time."

A November 1994 *NME* reported that Beatmaster V "didn't look in any way ill in Paris, held the beat down with relish, and contributed his fair share to the tour bus banter (mostly jokes at the expense of other group members)," before a recent diagnosis, and was "recovering as rapidly as could be hoped for," with plans to rejoin the tour.[3]

"We were on tour in Belgium, and they told me that Vic had leukemia," says Ice. "I cancelled the concert with a full house, and we got dragged for that. . . . We never told people he had cancer."

Shortly after recording drums for Body Count's third album, Beatmaster V died of leukemia on April 30, 1996. "He was the heartbeat of the band," says Ernie. Ice, who remembers not crying when either of his parents died ("To this day, I don't fully understand why.") recalled Beatmaster's funeral as the first time he cried in his adult life.[4]

[3]Fadele, Dele. "Ice-T: Seine in the Membrane." *New Musical Express*, November 12, 1994, https://www.rocksbackpages.com/library/article/ice-t -seine-in-the-membrane.

[4]Ice-T and Douglas Century. *Ice: A Memoir of Gangster Life and Redemption-from South Central to Hollywood*. United States, Random House Publishing Group, 2011.

Body Count's *Violent Demise: The Last Days* was released in 1997 and dedicated to Beatmaster V. By that time, Moose had left the band and been replaced by bassist Doug "Griz" Grigsby. "We were having internal conflicts with Moose," says Ernie, noting that the bassist moved to Lake Elsinore and was coming to rehearsal less. "He wanted to be in charge. And my personality is so laid back that he thought he could do a better job, but everybody knows how this ship runs. It runs a certain way."

"I told him he was out of the band. Vic my drummer says, 'I got my gun just in case he gets out of control,'" laughs Ernie.

Much of *Violent Demise* sounds like *Body Count* outtakes. Once more Body Count closes with a hair-raising title track, "Last Days," capping the record with an alarm-like riff beneath Ice's slam poetics, testifying that Body Count's last days might be all of ours. But *Violent Demise* seemed to confirm that *Body Count* was an outlier from a band that wouldn't catch lightning in a bottle again. Despite its release in the record industry's late-1990s peak, when it looked like any rapper with a rock band could get a record deal, *Violent Demise* went mostly unnoticed.

"Every time we would lose a member, we would try to regroup and try to keep the band alive," says Ice. "We struggled through the next albums."

Mooseman found a dream job in Iggy Pop's backing band, the Trolls, cowriting, and playing bass on Iggy's 2001 record *Beat 'Em Up*. On February 22, 2001, months before the album's release, Moose visited some friends in his old Rollin' 60s neighborhood in Los Angeles.

"He went back to his neighborhood, and was standing in the driveway with two friends, and a drive by shooting happens," says Ice. "He runs, he's the only one that gets shot. He's only one who's not gangbanging, and he's killed."

"Before he passed, I was gonna ask him to be back in the band. He grew up some. He was younger. Those few years of maturity have a lot to do with a person," says Ernie. "I was very sad when he got shot down there."

Body Count performed sporadically in the early 2000s, including some taped performances that were compiled, with some additional footage, for 2005's *Murder 4 Hire* video. (In a peak *Murder 4 Hire* moment, the band sign autographs for local policemen.) Ice also joined the Rollins Band for a scorching version of Black Flag's "Police Story" on 2002 album *Rise Above: 24 Black Flag Songs to Benefit the West Memphis Three*. "He gives it a real wallop," says Rollins. "He was a great asset to us in getting the album to people." Sadly, Body Count endured another tragedy before their next album release.

"D-Roc the Executioner, I saw him in a recording studio in North Hollywood. It was right before Christmas in 2002," says Long. "I'm like 'Yeah, man, I'm going home for Christmas vacation and we'll hang out when I get back.' And he kind of went, 'I don't know how much more hanging out I'm gonna be able to do, Hot Rod.' And I thought he was getting sober or something. I didn't know that he had already been diagnosed as terminal."

"We lost D-Roc to lymphoma. D-Roc always was sick, but I just didn't know how sick," says Ice. The guitarist died in August 2004 at the age of forty-five, at City of Hope hospital, leaving behind a daughter and a stepdaughter in Los Angeles.

"I was there that night he passed," says Ernie. *Murder 4 Hire* was dedicated to D-Roc's memory. "I hear about how we've been 'cursed' quite a bit," said Ernie. "I don't believe we've been cursed. I just believe we're Black men in America and the ratio for those kinds of things is a little higher for us than it is for everyone else."[5]

Body Count picked themselves up for 2006's *Murder 4 Hire* album, with bassist Vincent Price, a former Prince and Chris Cornell guitar tech from the band's rehearsal space, as well as guitarist Bendrix and drummer O.T. Ice calls it "the worst record." "The band wasn't even together," says Ice, who pasted vocals on tracks the musicians recorded in LA. "I don't even know if it came out through any label or nothing."

"After D-Roc passed I started drinking too much," says Ernie. "You get depressed, and you get sad and things like that. So I kind of lost track. And then you know how important or what you're doing means to people. People say, 'You got to do a record,' and this and that, and so then I was able to."

Ernie went to rehab and hasn't had a drink since 2010. "I work with MusiCares and I sit in a meeting every Tuesday," Ernie stated. "Young kids there are like, 'I want to be a rock star' and they're having trouble and I'm like, I'm a 58-year-

[5]Yoxheimer, Aaron. "Body Count: It's a Survivor." *The Morning Call*, October 5, 2021, https://www.mcall.com/news/mc-xpm-2007-03-31 -3708636-story.html.

old Black man in a speed metal band . . . come on you can do it, if I can!"[6]

"Every day pretty good, you know. I don't do bad days," says Ernie.

Other than a 2011 video game tie-in single for *Gears of War 3* (Ice voices a character), Body Count stopped touring and recording. Ice-T interviews focused more on *Law & Order* and his marriage to swimsuit model Coco Austin. "At that point, Body Count was over. I don't have my band members, I don't have anything," says Ice.

[6]Bianca. "Conversations with Bianca: Body Count + Bloodlust + Ice-T + Ernie C." May 29, 2017, http://conversationswithbianca.com/2017/05/29/body-count-ernie-c/.

12
"But tonight we get even."

"Coco was like, 'Why don't you start Body Count back?' I'm like, 'We can't, we need a label,'" says Ice. "Body Count is a lot of moving parts." But when approached by independent metal label Sumerian Records for a record deal, the band started to regroup.

"Vince got hold of Will, 'Ill Will' Dorsey who's from DC, who was a drummer, he'd been in playing a lot of punk bands. And then he got a hold of Juan, Juan of the Dead who was playing in groups like Evildead," says Ice. "Juan's Cuban, he got a gangsta look."

"Each person in the band right now is one person removed from the original person," says Ernie. "I can't replace Vic, but I can replace O.T. I can't replace D-Roc, but I can replace Bendrix . . . when Juan came into the band, all the pieces started to gel again."

"I've had seven variations of this band," says Ernie. "The only ones that have worked have been the first one and the one I have now. The five in the middle weren't the right combinations of people. . . . This band likes each other, we don't have any egos."

"Ernie wants to solo," says Ice. "I needed somebody that would play the rhythm and lock the main part of the song in so Ernie can jump on there with him."

"I do think they got inspired to find a sound that fit in with what was going on while still doing what they do. They were very, very open to the idea of, 'We don't have to do this band way we did 20 years ago,'" says producer Will Putney. "We could come up with new stuff and incorporate new things."

"We've been gone for almost ten years and no band has filled our spot," said Ice. "We just want to sound like ourselves, but better."[1]

Body Count rented a room in Las Vegas and started writing music together as a band. "Just like we did the first album," says Ice. "The first song we made was 'Talk Shit, Get Shot.'"

From the first seconds of "Talk Shit, Get Shot," Body Count have their catchiest song since their debut, as well as their biggest hit, thanks in part to a violent and comedic music video. The rest of the record holds up, from the hard-slamming murder fantasy "Pray for Death" to the pummeling "Back to Rehab" to the frenetic, whiplash-inducing tribute to women moshers, "Bitch in the Pit." *Manslaughter* scored another video hit with an uproarious update of Suicidal

---

[1]Dawes, Laina. "Body Count's Ice-T Talks Shit but Does the Shooting." *Decibel Magazine*, August 9, 2017, https://www.decibelmagazine.com/2014 /06/05/body-count-s-ice-t-talks-shit-but-does-the-shooting/.

Tendencies' "Institutionalized," remade with problems like Coco telling Ice he plays too much Xbox. Ice also takes his "99 Problems" hook back from Jay-Z, serving up the best of both versions by remaking Ice's original with hard-edged riffs in a Body Count stunner. "When this record comes out, a lot of fans will go, 'Oh that's Jay-Z,'" Ice stated. "And then their buddy gets to smack 'em in the face."[2]

Body Count regained their talent for immediate hooks, albeit with a new level of heaviness, putting Body Count back in contention for the world's greatest hardcore band. "When I heard 'Talk Shit, Get Shot,' I couldn't believe how well the music had translated, them working with Will Putney, modern production, bringing some connections to modern metalcore," says Doc Coyle.

McKagan brought his daughter to the *Manslaughter* tour. "She loved 'Bitch in the Pit' and all that stuff," says McKagan. "I'm like, 'These are my friends, you know.' 'Say what?'" He laughs. "It was fucking awesome, man, it was the first show back in LA. I guess the ban got taken off."

"They're threatening. I love that, when a band's threatening from stage," McKagan adds. "And I know these guys, right? But I'm still backing up a couple of steps, because I don't know what's going to happen."

That year, Body Count headlined a stage at Afropunk in Brooklyn, an annual music and arts festival described as "a

[2]Grow, Kory. "Ice-T Explains '99 Problems' and His Return to Body Count." *Rolling Stone*, June 12, 2014, https://www.rollingstone.com/music /music-news/ice-t-explains-why-he-remade-99-problems-and-brought -back-body-count-127177/.

voice for the unwritten, unwelcome and unheard of" that has expanded into "a global brand encompassing art, journalism, activism, and fashion with festivals in Atlanta, London, Paris and Johannesburg."[3] Watching the festival reach fans around the world, increasing the profile of Black punk and metal artists, one sees an international cultural sensation that celebrates the music and ideas Body Count pioneered on their first album.

"Part of being tough, being gangster, is saying, 'This is what I like and if you don't, if you got a problem with that, kiss my ass.' I don't think musical tastes have anything to do with race," says Ice. He brings up the rising punk-rap band Ho99o9. "They opened for us out here at one of our shows in New York. They were just two young cats wilding, they have a drummer . . . they rocked the fucking house," Ice emphasizes. "I was like, 'Man, go do what the fuck you do.'"

"Pick up an instrument, make your art," says Ice. "Don't allow other people to make you feel any kind of way about something you truly enjoy. Fuck them. And plus, if you're into metal, metal is pretty much 'fuck you,' you know what I'm saying? It is metal to be a Black kid liking metal."

"Be yourself. And come to a Body Count show," he laughs.

Ho99o9 spoke about their biggest influences for Records in My Life in 2017, with vocalist the OGM citing Body Count's debut first ("That shit's hardcore") before recounting Ho99o9's opening spot for Body Count at the Gramercy Theatre. "He was soundchecking when we walked in, and we

[3]Taylor, Leila. *Darkly: Blackness and America's Gothic Soul*. United States, Repeater, 2019.

were watching him, like, 'Oh my god, I can't believe that's Ice-T, he's really right there.' And he gets off the stage and he comes and shakes our hand. He says hello to us . . . . When we got off stage after he saw us perform, he rushes to the back room and he's just like, 'You motherfuckers are so crazy, are so insane. I love it. You guys should be called 'the Illmatics' because you're so ill.'"[4]

"Being Black and playing heavy metal, punk rock music, there wasn't a lot of us. Then these guys came around, and it was a whole different thing," says Price. "Other people would say, 'Oh you're white.' . . . Now it's everything's accepted, like when you see people wearing Metallica shirts, it's a fashion thing now. . . . But back then it was like, you're either this or you're that . . . to play with those guys, it's a good feeling."

"People look at it from the perspective of what that means for a mostly white fanbase to see that, but I think it actually means more to the Black community, when they see, especially a band like that where you got guys coming from the inner city, playing rock and metal," says Coyle. "It shows that culture that you're not bound to just do what is expected of you."

Body Count moved to Century Media for *Bloodlust* in 2017. It's even stronger than *Manslaughter*, kicking off with air raid sirens and a Dave Mustaine voiceover in "Civil War," before MegaDave lays down one of his untouchable

---

[4]"HO9O9 (Horror)—Records in My Life (2017 Interview)." *YouTube*, June 12, 2017, https://youtu.be/0HQL4lby0ps.

solos. *Bloodlust* features guests from more of metal's most recognizable voices, including Max Cavalera's bellow on "All Love Is Lost" and Randy Blythe's growl on "Walk with Me . . . ," but the album hits like 100% Body Count. The band draws on true crime (dropping an armed robbery into "The Ski Mask Way"), first-person horror scenarios ("Here I Go Again," "Bloodlust"), one of Body Count's most powerful street anthems and best videos ("This Is Why We Ride"), and even nailing one of the most daunting metal moves, a Slayer cover, with an ace "Raining Blood/ Postmortem" that's equal parts tribute and reinvention, with Ill Will's blast beats storming through the song's nonpareil progression while Ice and Vince step up on the mic. Best of all are *Bloodlust*'s sociopolitical songs. "No Lives Matter" and "Black Hoodie" are as explosive as hardcore music gets, musically and lyrically. "All these people out here tripping off police brutality, like this shit is something new? Give me a fucking break," Ice-T barks in "Black Hoodie," released on the twenty-fifth anniversary of *Body Count*.

"In this year of the rock protest song, there hasn't yet been a lyric as bitter, complex, and powerful as 'No Lives Matter.'" Robert Christgau reviewed *Bloodlust*. "You feel both a mind at work and an entertainer putting himself across."[5]

Remarkably, "Black Hoodie" was nominated for the 2018 Best Metal Performance Grammy. Body Count, once the scourge of conservative America, performed at the awards show, too brutal for the TV broadcast but watchable online,

[5]Christgau, Robert. *Robert Christgau: Dean of American Rock Critics*, https://www.robertchristgau.com/.

taking their police-tape-adorned stage set and blasting the Recording Academy insiders with the hardest set they'd see all night. The band played over the sound of gunfire, with Ice yelling "For Trayvon," and "For all the people killed by police," in the song's finale.[6] Body Count did not win the award that night, but they left with the most punk rock performance to ever make it to the Grammys stage.

Body Count cemented their rebirth with 2020's *Carnivore*, firing on all cylinders for a heavy groove metal album featuring Meshuggah-like tones and some of Ernie's best solos. The hard-charging single "Bum-Rush" makes an old chant sound refreshed by calling out modern American crises. Once more, some of Body Count's biggest metal peers lined up to work with them, like Slayer's Dave Lombardo on a thrashed-out "Colors," as did younger artists they've influenced, like Amy Lee on the Nipsey Hussle tribute "When I'm Gone." A version of Motörhead's "Ace of Spades" that had been blowing up the mosh pit at recent Body Count shows, especially when Ice sings upwards into the mic, Lemmy-style, makes its record debut. The album's heaviest song, the anti-police brutality "Point the Finger," was cowritten and performed with Riley Gale of Power Trip, an incredible young band with a heavy Body Count influence. "The title track of that record, holy shit, that's heavy as fuck," says Blythe. "I was bumping it heavy in the truck."

---

[6]"Body Count: 'Black Hoodie' Performance | 2018 Grammys." Recording Academy, https://www.grammy.com/videos/body-count-black-hoodie-performance-2018-grammys.

"They've always been amazing. But they're even now more amazing than ever, the musicianship level is fucking off the hook now," says Cavalera.

When touring plans for *Carnivore* were canceled in the COVID-19 pandemic, Body Count and Gale filmed and released a quarantined performance video for "Point the Finger," wilding out in their homes. By 2021, Ice was announcing work on the next Body Count record, *Merciless*, moving forward in the face of another adversity.

"Know your allies and let's continue to go forward. Don't let up. Let's go after Breonna Taylor's killers. Let's get it done," Ice told *The Washington Post*.[7]

At the March 2021 Grammys, *Carnivore* won the "Best Metal Performance" award for "Bum-Rush." In an acceptance speech filmed from home, Ice thanked Beatmaster V, Mooseman, and D-Roc along with his current bandmates. "Nelson George told me, 'People are like, 'Boycott it.' Nelson's like, 'That's what you do when you're 19.'" Ice stated on the hip-hop podcast *The Cipher*. "When you're 50something, you fucking go in there and take that motherfucking award and give it to your daughter."[8]

"There's something they can't take away," says Ernie. "It's there to say that Body Count is on the map as a metal band."

[7]Andrews-Dyer, Helena. "'Even Now the Line I'm Pushing May Not Be Radical Enough': Ice-T on Protests, Police Brutality and 'Cop Killer' 28 Years Later." *The Washington Post*, June 11, 2020.

[8]Setaro, Shawn. "230: Ice-T." *SoundCloud*, The Cipher, https://soundcloud.com/theciphershow/230-ice-t.

"I was really shocked," says Ill Will. "I had no words, I just shed a tear with my wife . . . it's been great."

Headbangers can point to the Grammys' history of bullshit, especially with metal. But the belated Grammy acknowledgment is more stunning, and shows Body Count's career arc, better than a cooler award like a *Decibel* Hall of Fame induction would. Body Count won the most mainstream, renowned music industry honor possible, almost thirty years after the US federal government, the gun lobby, and the US Police Force tried to shut them down. It's a victory that, in the words of Okayplayer's Gary Suarez, "affirms the work they've done, and continue to do, towards greater inclusivity for BIPOC listeners, and using metal to call out the injustices Black people face in America."[9] It's hard to think of a more astonishing comeback in punk or metal history.

[9]Suarez, Gary. "Why Ice-T's Body Count Grammy Award Win Matters." *Okayplayer*, March 16, 2021, https://www.okayplayer.com/music/ice-t-body -count-grammy-win-cop-killer.html.

13
"Body Count, motherfucker."

As of this writing, the original *Body Count* album is still not legally available in record stores or on streaming services. Despite rumors, no police officers were ever reported attacked or murdered through *Body Count's* influence. There has never been credible evidence that metal or rap causes violence, as opposed to the truth that the police have abused and killed more minorities than we will ever know. Banning "Cop Killer" didn't make the issues it addressed go away. But it also didn't take away Body Count's cathartic power.

"*Body Count* remains the most controversial metal record ever recorded and released for mass distribution (via Time Warner) and the only record to ever become a national legislative priority," wrote Invisible Oranges' Justin M. Norton. "It's the last time I remember when music seemed like a legitimate threat to social order."[1]

[1]Norton, Justin M. "Remembering 1992: The Summer of Body Count." *Invisible Oranges—The Metal Blog*, June 25, 2012, https://www.invisibleoranges.com/remembering-1992-the-summer-of-body-count/.

"Ice-T is still true to his game," says Angelo Moore. "He's just tapping into another part of the industry that he knows. Well, I mean, shit. He plays a cop. I'm sure he had to deal with a bunch of cops in real life. And not on the cops' side. But he knows what it is. He knows what they're all about. . . . When he puts together Body Count, he reminds everybody that he hasn't forgotten his culture and his people."

"With a movie, you're gonna get paid whether it sucks or not. TV is more stable. But there's nothing I've done that can compare to being on stage or being a rock star," Ice told *The Village Voice*.[2]

"You don't feel once that he became this kind of hipster TV guy, or a sold out rock metal guy. No, it's more like the opposite . . . . He gets to fund his dream, which is the metal, the Body Count," says Cavalera. "He's an iconic American personality. And he should be, man, because he's a treasure. He's an American treasure."

Ice-T has pioneered the idea of the rap entrepreneur, fulfilling his multimedia ambitions by crossing over into film, TV, books, video games, advertising, podcasting, and more, all while Body Count is thriving. The internet may have wreaked havoc on the music industry, but it leveled the playing field for Body Count, giving a song that was almost silenced by the government a new life. YouTube

---

[2]Turman, Katherine. "Body Count: 'Cop Killer' to Manslaughter." *The Village Voice*, May 11, 2017, https://www.villagevoice.com/2014/06/11/body-count-cop-killer-to-manslaughter/.

uploads of "Cop Killer" and *Body Count* each have over three million views, almost as many as newer songs like "No Lives Matter" and "Talk Shit, Get Shot." Ice-T himself is a particularly internet-friendly persona, a prolific social media presence who reaches new fans with his professional shit-talker deftness. Decades after the President of the United States called his music "sick" and "filth," America elected a President who wanted to shake Ice-T's hand and get a picture with him, onetime *Law & Order* guest star Joe Biden. "In the middle of the scene he just yells out 'Where's Ice-T?'" Ice says. "I'm like, 'Oh shit!'"

Ernie reflects on the "Cop Killer" maelstrom. "That was a momentum-killer," he says. "But you know, that's why we're still here to this day. . . . A lot of bands of that era there aren't around because they stood for nothing. They were just, 'We're gonna go party, we're gonna get high, we're gonna get drunk.' We stood for something and we stuck by our guns and we've been very consistent with our message."

"Without tarnishing the brand of them being unapproachable and scary, they are honestly some of the sweetest guys I know," says Putney. "I wouldn't cross them, for sure. But they're definitely good guys to have on your team."

Body Count are more celebrated now than they've ever been. In 2020, *Spin*'s "50 Best Rock Bands Right Now" feature honored Body Count for their "volatile brew of social realism and sociopathic fantasy, class analysis and moral trolling," and for giving "our more-Reagan-than-Reagan era the more-gangsta-than-gangsta soundtrack it badly needs."[3] Body Count are also now a music festival staple at everything from Ozzfest to Afropunk to Download to Wacken. "I want to get new fans and play in the afternoon amongst all newer bands, and try to build a new fan base of young kids," said Ice. "We know what the fuck we're doing."[4]

But even if Body Count never made another good record, their debut would keep them relevant. *Body Count* sounds more pertinent by the month, a brick through the window of America's suburbs that stayed embedded in the hearts and minds of headbangers everywhere. Body Count pioneered a sound that would find worldwide success yet never match the original's potency. Body Count's music and ideologies are seen in the rise of cultural movements like Afropunk and political movements like Black Lives Matter, based on the kind of work Body Count was persecuted for in the 1990s. The themes of songs like "Body Count," "There Goes the Neighborhood," "Bowels of the Devil," "The Winner Loses," and "Cop Killer" are a bigger part of the world's cultural conversation than they've ever been, as are more recent Body Count songs, like "No Lives Matter," "Black Hoodie," and "Point the Finger."

"The first set of members hit the mark so hard to where the group that we have now are able to go forward," says Sean. "Their work was so good that we were able to build

[3]*Spin* staff. "The 50 Best Rock Bands Right Now." *Spin*, July 20, 2020, https://www.spin.com/2020/07/the-50-best-rock-bands-right-now-2020/.

[4]Dawes, Laina. "Body Count's Ice-T Talks Shit but Does the Shooting." *Decibel Magazine*, June 5, 2014, https://www.decibelmagazine.com/2014/06/05/body-count-s-ice-t-talks-shit-but-does-the-shooting/.

on it and carry on today. But if it wasn't for what they did on that first run, we probably wouldn't be here right now. . . . The foundation they were built on is just some real stuff."

The lyrics are specific enough to define its era and broad enough to be significant now. *Body Count* gives metal a hardcore rawness, with heavy, distorted tones that make its imitators sound like pop-punk. It sounds imitable, yet it remains unmatched, an array of moods with instant hooks built on the chemistry of five high school friends who grew into a powerhouse metal band.

"It was more like [Bob Marley's] 'I Shot the Sheriff,'" Ernie described "Cop Killer" to *Billboard*. "A rally song for people with no voices that were able to scream 'Fuck the police!' at the top of their lungs."[5]

Those voices are raised at Body Count shows, where "Cop Killer" is the band's most-performed song. As far back as 1991, Body Count have been ending shows with "Cop Killer." "All rise for the new national anthem," Ice-T introduces the song, decades after he defended it by comparing "Cop Killer" to "The Star-Spangled Banner." Ernie closes by playing his guitar upside down, like the burning guitar in the "There Goes the Neighborhood" video.

"We pulled the song to say, 'It's not about money. It's about these cops,'" says Ernie. "We didn't make money on it. We just made our point. And we got our point across."

[5]Knopper, Steve. "Nearly 30 Years Later, Body Count's 'Cop Killer' Remains Absent from Streaming - What Happened?" *Billboard*, 11 June 2020, https://www.billboard.com/music/rb-hip-hop/ice-t-body-count-cop-killer -streaming-9400752/.

"Racism is part of America's fabric. You start with the Native Americans, Blacks and go on. Racism is part of the world, but a lot of damage is done here in the United States. I think KRS-One said it best, 'you'll never have justice on stolen land.' After what I've seen this year, though, it gives me a lot of hope because a lot of it was brought to the forefront. When I saw the diversity in the Black Lives Matter marches, as much as people tried to demonize and say they were a terrorist group and all that bullshit, it gave me hope," Ice stated in a 2020 interview. "I think the youngsters are going to be activists and they are going to fight to make the change that's needed in the next hundred years."[6]

"We're still dealing with police brutality," says Ice. "We're still dealing with racism, 'Momma's Gotta Die Tonight.' We're still dealing with all the bullshit that we sung about."

"I'm quite sure there's still a voodoo bitch down in New Orleans," he laughs. "KKK bitch is still down south in Georgia."

"I think all artists are looking for the term 'classic,'" says Ice. "'There's a Dead Kennedys record you've got to hear, this is the Black Flag album you need to get,' so you're hoping to get a classic album. And the 'Cop Killer' album will always be our classic."

"That's the record I worked my whole life to do," stated Ernie. "I worked 30 years to create that record."[7]

[6]Godla, Frank. "Ice T Talks Body Count Fans, What the Grammys Are Really like, the Current State of Racism & More." *Metal Injection*, December 22, 2020, https://metalinjection.net/interviews/ice-t-talks-body-count-fans-what-the-grammys-are-really-like-the-current-state-of-racism-more.

[7]Pementel, Michael. "Body Count's Ernie C Talks Playing Video Games with Lemmy & 30th Anniversary of the Band's Debut Album." The Pit, July

Body Count is available for anyone who wants to blow off steam, or trace the origins of Afropunk and metalcore. It's there for anyone who wants to throw up the horns for some screamalong, riff-heavy thrash, or to find out what record was powerful enough to set off nationwide protests, jeopardize the stock price of the world's biggest media conglomerate, and provoke the President of the United States into putting his foot down. It's there for anyone who wants to mosh, laugh, or vent. It's there for anyone raging against some of America's worst tendencies and deeply entrenched institutions.

"Body Count's a part of the grass that's growing from the shit that's been happening in our country for the past three to four hundred years," says Moore. "Fishbone, Living Colour, Bad Brains, all these Black rock bands that talk about racism, or talk about their disgust in how the system is run."

"They've been very relevant everywhere on the planet, especially places where there are a lot of real hard situations, war torn situations," says Chuck D.

"We still got a lot more to say. I know Ice has a lot more to say," says Ill Will. "People are surprised. They say, 'Hold on, Ice-T's singing this?' . . . I love that reaction, man."

"We're making some actual commentary, and we're living in such a socially active environment right now," says Ice. "That's where Body Count thrives."

On stage, the songs are more vicious than ever, gaining urgency as more police brutality and white supremacy come

2, 2022, https://www.wearethepit.com/2022/06/body-counts-ernie-c-talks -hanging-with-lemmy-anniversary-of-debut-lp/.

to light in the United States. *Body Count* is heavy enough to bring its most outlandish humor to life and make the most powerful forces it attacks feel threatened. It sounds learnable and writable enough to spark action.

Body Count outlasted the politicians that scorned them and the record stores that banned them. The PMRC has folded and the NRA has filed for bankruptcy. Jack Thompson was permanently disbarred in 2008. But Body Count are still confronting racism, police misconduct, mass incarceration, and political corruption, outliving their old adversaries and striking out at new ones. Ice's *Rolling Stone* cover and story are now emblazoned on a wall at the Rock and Roll Hall of Fame Museum in Cleveland, saluted as a fighter for free speech. A photograph of Ernie and Ice on stage together is enshrined in the Smithsonian's collection for the National Museum of African American History and Culture in Washington, D.C. And Body Count are still annihilating every town they visit, opening up the most ferocious mosh pits your venue will ever see. They're here, they ain't going nowhere, they're moving right next door to you.

"I don't know how you could make a record bigger than that," Ice stated. "That motherfucking record stopped the world."[8] *Body Count* always does, and will for the ages.

[8]Rowley, Scott. "The Record That Stopped the World: The Outrage and the Comedy behind Body Count's Cop Killer." *Metal Hammer*, June 1, 2020, https://www.loudersound.com/features/body-count-story-behind-cop-killer.

Body Count

"Smoked Pork"

> Ernie: "Ice was just doing a lot of talking stuff. We didn't
> know that was going to be organized like that."
>
> Ice: "It's just me walking up and shooting a cop (laughs).
> But it's done tongue in cheek. . . . Body Count is to be
> taken with a grain of salt."

"Body Count's in the House"

> Ernie: "That line is taken off 'Godzilla,' you know,
> (hums Blue Öyster Cult's 'Godzilla'). . . . It was kind
> of meant to remind you of that. It was going to be
> an introduction to let everyone who's the band. It's
> like an old R&B show, that's the way bands would
> talk, 'This is so and so, and this is so and so.' . . . We
> brought that kind of R&B thing into rock 'n' roll."
>
> Ice: "I always liked when Suicidal would have people
> chanting (sings Suicidal Tendencies' 'Pledge Your
> Allegiance') 'ST, ST.' . . . So I wanted to make a song
> that would make people actually say the name of the
> band and really drill the name of the band into their

heads. . . . I wanted to have a song to introduce us at a concert."

"Now Sports"

Ice: "'Now Sports' is where the term 'body count' came from . . . I was like, 'Wow, this is really who we are. We're just a body count.'"

"Body Count"

Ernie: "The song wasn't originally written like that. We did all the parts and at the end it went to that Hendrix slow vamp (hums it.) I'm playing that raised ninth chord that's kind of in the middle of it. That was gonna be at the end. But the engineer rewound it too fast, and so he skipped over and put the parts in the wrong part. . . . So after we listened to it we're like, 'That sounds pretty good!'"

Ice: "I think that song encapsulates what the group is about still today. It's about Black voices yelling at the top of their lungs about topics and don't give me no bullshit."

"A Statistic"

Ice: "That's just a rough statistic . . . that's a fucked-up statistic."

"Bowels of the Devil"

Ernie: "'Bowels of the Devil,' these are just fast kind of punk lines that we had. And so Ice, we did all the

music and then he just kind of wrote it. It just came
together really fast and came together really good."

Ice: "'Bowels of the Devil' is a song about being stuck
in prison and how they will take your life and what
prison really is. It's basically the warning sign . . .
'going out the back door,' that's a term for dying in
prison."

"The Real Problem"

Ice: "I don't even remember that song."

"KKK Bitch"

Ernie: "Another one of those simple punk songs that
were easy to write, it's like 1-3-5, almost like blues
progressions. Everything on that first record was kind
of bluesy and had a blues feel to it."

Ice: "This is Body Count in full effect, making fun of
a serious topic. When we would tour we'd go down
south and all the little white girls was definitely
jocking. But then when you ask them about their
family members, they're like, 'Oh, yeah, my brother or
my father, he don't like Black people.' I'm like, 'that's
why you're backstage, huh?' So we just took it to the
next level of thinking that their parent might be the
leader of the KKK."

"C Note"

Ernie: "'C Note' was just that I was sitting around
in the studio one night, and I was just, I played
those chords and I'm like, 'Okay, let me play on

top of it.' And then played through some kind of harmonizer. . . . I let Ice hear it the next day or something like that. And he's like, 'That's badass,' so we kept it."

Ice: "It's just Ernie wanting to play his guitar and letting him do his thing . . . the band is based around Ernie C, so if he wants a solo, he gets a solo."

"Voodoo"

Ernie: "'Voodoo' was a song we were working out in the studio, then our friend, Pimpin' Rex came and he started talking about the 'voodoo,' that's where Ice got the idea because he was like 'This band has this voodoo to it,' talking about the band had voodoo, so Ice kind of wrote that song around it."

Ice: "It's an outrageous song about me going down to New Orleans meeting some voodoo bitch, who starts stabbing a doll and fucking me up. Nothing more than that, (laughs) it's intentionally violent, but it's also very humorous."

"The Winner Loses"

Ernie: "I did that as a demo, before Body Count, I sang on it. It was about a friend of ours named Michael Bivins. And not Michael Bivins from Bel Biv Devoe, but we had a friend named Michael Bivins who was taking drugs. At the end the guy dies, but Michael Bivins is still alive today. That's probably my favorite guitar solo that I've ever done. It's the longest one, it was like an Ernie Isley-type of long solo and I was able to have some melody too, and some finger stuff, like a whole bunch of different styles on in that solo."

Ice: "It's a sincere song about people on drugs and having a friend that has always been winning but drugs will take you down . . . he basically might have helped kill his friend, so that's a very serious song."

"There Goes the Neighborhood"

Ernie: "'There Goes the Neighborhood,' that's just a lot of fun . . . we were trying to find a way to put that in, that little finger thing in the middle of it. . . . That song had a lot of different guitar parts. And we just put a whole lot of different guitar things that worked. And it all worked on that song."

Ice: "'There Goes the Neighborhood' is just a song of us coming into the rock world where all of a sudden they see Black band members. It's funny, now we're still on tour and people will see us backstage and they might not recognize some of my guys and they think they're the driver or something. There's not that many Black people in heavy metal or in the rock community. So when we did come in, and we fucking really dominated and kicked ass, that's what they said. And that's the term when the Black people move into the neighborhood. 'Oh, there goes the neighborhood.' So the neighborhood in this song was rock 'n' roll music."

"Oprah"

Ice: "I don't even remember that."

"Evil Dick"

> Ernie: "'Evil Dick,' (laughs) that was like an anthem song
> for a while. It was like a Body Count anthem. It's just
> a fun song. When the band first came out, that first
> record has a good sense of humor to it. That second
> record doesn't have a sense of humor, because we
> went through so much crap. . . . But the first record
> was just a fun, sense of humor, party record."

> Ice: "I'm saying that we got two heads, we have one head
> that says one thing and then your dick has its own
> brain. So in that song, I turned Evil Dick into a person
> that's telling you 'Don't sleep alone, don't sleep alone.'
> It's a song about a person's fight between his brain and
> his dick. (Laughs)"

"Body Count Anthem"

> Ernie: "'Body Count Anthem' was just an instrumental.
> . . . We used to rehearse and try to do new sharp
> stops and things like that . . . it was going to be our
> introduction song. So it was just what the band played
> when Ice wasn't around."

> Ice: "'Body Count Anthem' was much like the opening
> song, 'Body Count's in the House.' It's just a chance to
> get the audience to scream 'Body Count.'"

"Momma's Gotta Die Tonight"

> Ernie: "I like the way that song grooves. I like that groove
> better than almost any record that we've done. The
> way it comes in, the way Moose comes in kind of late.

It was a little bit behind the guitars, he's not on top of 'em, he's not playing the exact parts, he's playing a little bit behind to make it sound like it's lagging, like you're low-riding in it. I like that. . . . I think it's the smoothest guitar solo I've ever done."

Ice: "'Momma' is just a metaphor for racism. It means it has to be dismantled and taken apart. And 'Momma's Gotta Die Tonight' is a good example of Body Count. Because once again, it's not meant to be taken literally. . . . I just have fun making these types of songs."

"Out in the Parking Lot"

Ice: "That's just me talking shit, just saying that I hate racist cops so much that I'd like to hurt 'em."

"Cop Killer"

Ernie: "Everything all came together on that song. It's still back to the simple punk beat, and by being so simple, it makes it easy for the message to get through . . . it's kind of just a regular chorus verse, chorus verse, real simple, like that breakdown, a real uncomplicated song."

Ice: "We wrote the song, little did I know this guy would be some type of hero because people were so angry at police injustice. . . . We actually thought 'Momma's Gotta Die Tonight' would be the most controversial."

Gotta lotta love

Acknowledgments with "My friends and family, Leah Babb-Rosenfeld, Sean Maloney, Rachel Moore, the master D.X. Ferris, Pam Nashel and Taylor Haughton at Siren's Call, Matt Wardlaw and Annie Zaleski, Ben and Matt, Rob and Frank, Eric at Booked on Rock, Corey at SongFacts, Tim and Eric at Somewhere in Time, Nick Spacek at *The Pitch*, Ryan Downey at Speak N' Destroy, Brian Hardzinski and Madeleine Brand at KCRW, Mik Davis at T-Bones Records and Cafe, Pete Gulyas at Blue Arrow Records, Teddy Wayne, Giles Brown, Vishnu Prasad, Benedict O'Hagan, Molly Walsh, Sylvia Panth, Rob Sheffield, Michael Stiglitz, William Lent, Lucky 13 Saloon, Andy, Billy and Pat in Eat, Kyle and Brenda, the best ever death metal kids from Virginia, Jesse Rifkin, Gaby Moss, Word Bookstore, Saint Vitus, public libraries (Brooklyn, New York, Queens, Newark, and Thompson), Griz, O.T., Bendrix, Sean E. Mac, Body Count fans all over the world, Anne-Marie Anderson, Jello Biafra, Lorrie Boula, Bobby Brooks, Gloria Cavalera, Max Cavalera, Dan Charnas, Doc Coyle, Heidi Siegmund Cuda, Chuck D, Laina Dawes, Ron DeLord, Warren Drummond, Jon Freeman, Corey Glover, Dave Halili, David Harleston, Gibby Haynes, Gary Holt, Howie Klein, Chris "Hot Rod" Long, Matt Mahurin, Michaelangelo Matos, Bernard Matthews, Bob Merlis, Angelo Moore, Darlene Ortiz, Phyllis Pollack, Will Putney, Vernon Reid, Henry Rollins, Angie Seegers, Shawn Setaro, Barry Shank, Troy Staton, Steve Stewart, Bram Teitelman, Katherine Turman, Jean-Claude Van Damme, Zane Warman, Ulrich Wild, Juan Williams, Sean Yseult, Mark Zonder, and of course Jorge Hinojosa, Juan of the Dead, Vincent Price, Ill Will, Sean E. Sean, Ice-T, and Ernie C, with eternal gratitude for D-Roc the Executioner, Mooseman, and Beatmaster V."

A Speedy T's heart formation for Michelle Campagna, who told me she wasn't a metalhead when we met but called "Cop Killer" "a great song" within the first year.

"In token of my admiration for his genius, this book is inscribed to Ilja Wachs."

Selected Bibliography

Academic journals

Academy of Criminal Justice Sciences
Journal of Communication Inquiry
Race & Class

Books

Austin, Joe, and Michael Nevin Willard. *Generations of Youth: Youth Cultures and History in Twentieth-Century America*. United States, New York University Press, 1998.

Blecha, Peter. *Taboo Tunes: A History of Banned Bands & Censored Songs*. United States, Backbeat Books, 2004.

Bryant, Jerry H. *Born in a Mighty Bad Land the Violent Man in African American Folklore and Fiction*. United States, Indiana University Press, 2003.

Chang, Jeff. *Can't Stop Won't Stop: A History of the Hip-Hop Generation*. United States, St. Martin's Press, 2007.

Charnas, Dan. *The Big Payback: The History of the Business of Hip-Hop*. United States, New American Library, 2011.

Dawes, Laina. *What Are You Doing Here?: A Black Woman's Life and Liberation in Heavy Metal.* United States, Bazillion Points, 2020.

Dylan, Bob. *Bob Dylan Chronicles: Volume One.* Simon & Schuster, 2004.

Ice-T and Douglas Century. *Ice: A Memoir of Gangster Life and Redemption-from South Central to Hollywood.* United States, Random House Publishing Group, 2011.

Ice-T and Heidi Siegmund Cuda. *The Ice Opinion: Who Gives a Fuck?* United States, St. Martin's Press, 1994.

Ice-T, et al. *Split Decision: Life Stories.* United States, Gallery Books, 2022.

Mahon, Maureen. *Right to Rock: The Black Rock Coalition and the Cultural Politics of Race.* United States, Duke University Press, 2004.

Metcalf, Josephine, and Will Turner. *Rapper, Writer, Pop-Cultural Player: Ice-T and the Politics of Black Cultural Production.* United Kingdom, Routledge, 2016.

Ortiz, Darlene, and Heidi Siegmund Cuda. *Definition of Down: My Life with Ice T & the Birth of Hip Hop.* United States, Over the Edge Books, 2015.

Perkins, William Eric. *Droppin' Science: Critical Essays on Rap Music and Hip Hop Culture.* United States, Temple University Press, 1996.

Taylor, Leila. *Darkly: Blackness and America's Gothic Soul.* United States, Repeater, 2019.

Walser, Robert. *Running with the Devil: Power, Gender, and Madness in Heavy Metal Music.* United States, Wesleyan University Press, 2014.

Westhoff, Ben. *Original Gangstas: Tupac Shakur, Dr. Dre, Eazy-E, Ice Cube, and the Birth of West Coast Rap.* United States, Hachette Books, 2017.

Film

Body Count: Live in L.A. Performance by Body Count, Escapi Music, 2005.

Body Count: Murder 4 Hire. Directed by Erik Voake, Woodhaven Entertainment, 2005.

Hail! Hail! Rock 'n' Roll. Directed by Taylor Hackford, Universal, 1987.

Iceberg Slim: Portrait of a Pimp. Directed by Jorge Hinojosa, Final Level Entertainment, 2012.

Let It Fall: Los Angeles 1982–1992. Directed by John Ridley, ABC Studios, 2017.

Something from Nothing: The Art of Rap. Directed by Ice-T, Final Level Entertainment, 2012.

Smoke Out Festival Presents Body Count Featuring Ice-T. Directed by Brian Lockwood, Eagle Rock Entertainment, 2005.

Magazines

The Aquarian

The Atlantic

Axcess

BAM

Billboard

Columbia Journalism Review

Creem

Decibel

Entertainment Weekly

Esquire

GQ

Guitar World

Jet

Kerrang!
Loudwire
Melody Maker
Metal Hammer
Musician
Newsweek
NME
Premier Guitar
Q
Recovery Today
Revolver
Rolling Stone
Slate
Spin
Time
Variety
Vibe
The Village Voice
The Wire

News Services

Associated Press
CBC News
MTV News
Reuters
United Press International

Newspapers

The Boston Globe
Chicago Tribune

Los Angeles Times
The Morning Call
The New York Times
News & Record
The Ottawa Citizen
Tampa Bay Times
The Seattle Times
The Washington Post

Podcasts

Appetite for Distortion
The Cipher
Conversations with Bianca
The Ex-Man with Doc Coyle
The Official Danko Jones Podcast
Questlove Supreme
Sound Vapors
WTF with Marc Maron

Radio

NPR
WQXR

Television

In Living Color
The Jimmy Lloyd Songwriter Showcase
MTV Rockumentary

Origins of Hip-Hop
Rockline on MTV
Rolling Stone: Stories from the Edge
The Whoopi Goldberg Show
Without Walls

Websites

American Archive of Public Broadcasting
American Presidency Project
Blabbermouth.net
Body Count Corner
C-Span.org
Grammy.com
Invisible Oranges
JimShelley.com
Loudersound
Metal Injection
MetalSucks
Mike Zeck Checklist
MusicRadar
Okayplayer
The Pit
Red Bull Music Academy
RobertChristgau.com
Rock's Backpages
YouTube

Some interviews have been edited and condensed for clarity.

Also Available in the Series

1. *Dusty Springfield's Dusty in Memphis* by Warren Zanes
2. *Love's Forever Changes* by Andrew Hultkrans
3. *Neil Young's Harvest* by Sam Inglis
4. *The Kinks' The Kinks Are the Village Green Preservation Society* by Andy Miller
5. *The Smiths' Meat Is Murder* by Joe Pernice
6. *Pink Floyd's The Piper at the Gates of Dawn* by John Cavanagh
7. *ABBA's ABBA Gold: Greatest Hits* by Elisabeth Vincentelli
8. *The Jimi Hendrix Experience's Electric Ladyland* by John Perry
9. *Joy Division's Unknown Pleasures* by Chris Ott
10. *Prince's Sign "☉" the Times* by Michaelangelo Matos
11. *The Velvet Underground's The Velvet Underground & Nico* by Joe Harvard
12. *The Beatles' Let It Be* by Steve Matteo
13. *James Brown's Live at the Apollo* by Douglas Wolk
14. *Jethro Tull's Aqualung* by Allan Moore
15. *Radiohead's OK Computer* by Dai Griffiths
16. *The Replacements' Let It Be* by Colin Meloy
17. *Led Zeppelin's Led Zeppelin IV* by Erik Davis
18. *The Rolling Stones' Exile on Main St.* by Bill Janovitz
19. *The Beach Boys' Pet Sounds* by Jim Fusilli
20. *Ramones' Ramones* by Nicholas Rombes
21. *Elvis Costello's Armed Forces* by Franklin Bruno
22. *R.E.M.'s Murmur* by J. Niimi

23. *Jeff Buckley's Grace* by Daphne Brooks

24. *DJ Shadow's Endtroducing.....* by Eliot Wilder

25. *MC5's Kick Out the Jams* by Don McLeese

26. *David Bowie's Low* by Hugo Wilcken

27. *Bruce Springsteen's Born in the U.S.A.* by Geoffrey Himes

28. *The Band's Music from Big Pink* by John Niven

29. *Neutral Milk Hotel's In the Aeroplane over the Sea* by Kim Cooper

30. *Beastie Boys' Paul's Boutique* by Dan Le Roy

31. *Pixies' Doolittle* by Ben Sisario

32. *Sly and the Family Stone's There's a Riot Goin' On* by Miles Marshall Lewis

33. *The Stone Roses' The Stone Roses* by Alex Green

34. *Nirvana's In Utero* by Gillian G. Gaar

35. *Bob Dylan's Highway 61 Revisited* by Mark Polizzotti

36. *My Bloody Valentine's Loveless* by Mike McGonigal

37. *The Who's The Who Sell Out* by John Dougan

38. *Guided by Voices' Bee Thousand* by Marc Woodworth

39. *Sonic Youth's Daydream Nation* by Matthew Stearns

40. *Joni Mitchell's Court and Spark* by Sean Nelson

41. *Guns N' Roses' Use Your Illusion I and II* by Eric Weisbard

42. *Stevie Wonder's Songs in the Key of Life* by Zeth Lundy

43. *The Byrds' The Notorious Byrd Brothers* by Ric Menck

44. *Captain Beefheart's Trout Mask Replica* by Kevin Courrier

45. *Minutemen's Double Nickels on the Dime* by Michael T. Fournier

46. *Steely Dan's Aja* by Don Breithaupt

47. *A Tribe Called Quest's People's Instinctive Travels and the Paths of Rhythm* by Shawn Taylor

48. *PJ Harvey's Rid of Me* by Kate Schatz

49. *U2's Achtung Baby* by Stephen Catanzarite

50. *Belle & Sebastian's If You're Feeling Sinister* by Scott Plagenhoef

51. *Nick Drake's Pink Moon* by Amanda Petrusich

52. *Celine Dion's Let's Talk About Love* by Carl Wilson

53. *Tom Waits' Swordfishtrombones* by David Smay

54. *Throbbing Gristle's 20 Jazz Funk Greats* by Drew Daniel

55. *Patti Smith's Horses* by Philip Shaw

56. *Black Sabbath's Master of Reality* by John Darnielle

57. *Slayer's Reign in Blood* by D.X. Ferris

58. *Richard and Linda Thompson's Shoot Out the Lights* by Hayden Childs

59. *The Afghan Whigs' Gentlemen* by Bob Gendron

60. *The Pogues' Rum, Sodomy, and the Lash* by Jeffery T. Roesgen

61. *The Flying Burrito Brothers' The Gilded Palace of Sin* by Bob Proehl

62. *Wire's Pink Flag* by Wilson Neate

63. *Elliott Smith's XO* by Mathew Lemay

64. *Nas' Illmatic* by Matthew Gasteier

65. *Big Star's Radio City* by Bruce Eaton

66. *Madness' One Step Beyond…* by Terry Edwards

67. *Brian Eno's Another Green World* by Geeta Dayal

68. *The Flaming Lips' Zaireeka* by Mark Richardson

69. *The Magnetic Fields' 69 Love Songs* by LD Beghtol

70. *Israel Kamakawiwo'ole's Facing Future* by Dan Kois

71. *Public Enemy's It Takes a Nation of Millions to Hold Us Back* by Christopher R. Weingarten

72. *Pavement's Wowee Zowee* by Bryan Charles

73. *AC/DC's Highway to Hell* by Joe Bonomo

74. *Van Dyke Parks's Song Cycle* by Richard Henderson

75. *Slint's Spiderland* by Scott Tennent

76. *Radiohead's Kid A* by Marvin Lin

77. *Fleetwood Mac's Tusk* by Rob Trucks

78. *Nine Inch Nails' Pretty Hate Machine* by Daphne Carr

79. *Ween's Chocolate and Cheese* by Hank Shteamer

80. *Johnny Cash's American Recordings* by Tony Tost

81. *The Rolling Stones' Some Girls* by Cyrus Patell

82. *Dinosaur Jr.'s You're Living All Over Me* by Nick Attfield

83. *Television's Marquee Moon* by Bryan Waterman

84. *Aretha Franklin's Amazing Grace* by Aaron Cohen

85. *Portishead's Dummy* by RJ Wheaton

86. *Talking Heads' Fear of Music* by Jonathan Lethem

87. *Serge Gainsbourg's Histoire de Melody Nelson* by Darran Anderson

88. *They Might Be Giants' Flood* by S. Alexander Reed and Elizabeth Sandifer

89. *Andrew W.K.'s I Get Wet* by Phillip Crandall

90. *Aphex Twin's Selected Ambient Works Volume II* by Marc Weidenbaum

91. *Gang of Four's Entertainment* by Kevin J.H. Dettmar

92. *Richard Hell and the Voidoids' Blank Generation* by Pete Astor

93. *J Dilla's Donuts* by Jordan Ferguson

94. *The Beach Boys' Smile* by Luis Sanchez

95. *Oasis' Definitely Maybe* by Alex Niven

96. *Liz Phair's Exile in Guyville* by Gina Arnold

97. *Kanye West's My Beautiful Dark Twisted Fantasy* by Kirk Walker Graves

98. *Danger Mouse's The Grey Album* by Charles Fairchild

99. *Sigur Rós's ()* by Ethan Hayden

100. *Michael Jackson's Dangerous* by Susan Fast

101. *Can's Tago Mago* by Alan Warner

102. *Bobbie Gentry's Ode to Billie Joe* by Tara Murtha

103. *Hole's Live Through This* by Anwen Crawford

104. *Devo's Freedom of Choice* by Evie Nagy

105. *Dead Kennedys' Fresh Fruit for Rotting Vegetables* by Michael Stewart Foley

106. *Koji Kondo's Super Mario Bros.* by Andrew Schartmann

107. *Beat Happening's Beat Happening* by Bryan C. Parker

108. *Metallica's Metallica* by David Masciotra

109. *Phish's A Live One* by Walter Holland

110. *Miles Davis' Bitches Brew* by George Grella Jr.

111. *Blondie's Parallel Lines* by Kembrew McLeod

112. *Grateful Dead's Workingman's Dead* by Buzz Poole

113. *New Kids On The Block's Hangin' Tough* by Rebecca Wallwork

114. *The Geto Boys' The Geto Boys* by Rolf Potts

115. *Sleater-Kinney's Dig Me Out* by Jovana Babovic

116. *LCD Soundsystem's Sound of Silver* by Ryan Leas

117. *Donny Hathaway's Donny Hathaway Live* by Emily J. Lordi

118. *The Jesus and Mary Chain's Psychocandy* by Paula Mejia

119. *The Modern Lovers' The Modern Lovers* by Sean L. Maloney

120. *Angelo Badalamenti's Soundtrack from Twin Peaks* by Clare Nina Norelli

121. *Young Marble Giants' Colossal Youth* by Michael Blair and Joe Bucciero

122. *The Pharcyde's Bizarre Ride II the Pharcyde* by Andrew Barker

123. *Arcade Fire's The Suburbs* by Eric Eidelstein

124. *Bob Mould's Workbook* by Walter Biggins and Daniel Couch

125. *Camp Lo's Uptown Saturday Night* by Patrick Rivers and Will Fulton

126. *The Raincoats' The Raincoats* by Jenn Pelly

127. *Björk's Homogenic* by Emily Mackay

128. *Merle Haggard's Okie from Muskogee* by Rachel Lee Rubin

129. *Fugazi's In on the Kill Taker* by Joe Gross

130. *Jawbreaker's 24 Hour Revenge Therapy* by Ronen Givony

131. *Lou Reed's Transformer* by Ezra Furman

132. *Siouxsie and the Banshees' Peepshow* by Samantha Bennett

133. *Drive-By Truckers' Southern Rock Opera* by Rien Fertel

134. *dc Talk's Jesus Freak* by Will Stockton and D. Gilson

135. *Tori Amos's Boys for Pele* by Amy Gentry

136. *Odetta's One Grain of Sand* by Matthew Frye Jacobson

137. *Manic Street Preachers' The Holy Bible* by David Evans

138. *The Shangri-Las' Golden Hits of the Shangri-Las* by Ada Wolin

139. *Tom Petty's Southern Accents* by Michael Washburn

140. *Massive Attack's Blue Lines* by Ian Bourland

141. *Wendy Carlos's Switched-On Bach* by Roshanak Kheshti

142. *The Wild Tchoupitoulas' The Wild Tchoupitoulas* by Bryan Wagner

143. *David Bowie's Diamond Dogs* by Glenn Hendler

144. *D'Angelo's Voodoo* by Faith A. Pennick

145. *Judy Garland's Judy at Carnegie Hall* by Manuel Betancourt

146. *Elton John's Blue Moves* by Matthew Restall

147. *Various Artists' I'm Your Fan: The Songs of Leonard Cohen* by Ray Padgett

148. *Janet Jackson's The Velvet Rope* by Ayanna Dozier

149. *Suicide's Suicide* by Andi Coulter

150. *Elvis Presley's From Elvis in Memphis* by Eric Wolfson

151. *Nick Cave and the Bad Seeds' Murder Ballads* by Santi Elijah Holley

152. *24 Carat Black's Ghetto: Misfortune's Wealth* by Zach Schonfeld

153. *Carole King's Tapestry* by Loren Glass

154. *Pearl Jam's Vs.* by Clint Brownlee

155. *Roxy Music's Avalon* by Simon Morrison

156. *Duran Duran's Rio* by Annie Zaleski

157. *Donna Summer's Once Upon a Time* by Alex Jeffery

158. *Sam Cooke's Live at the Harlem Square Club, 1963* by Colin Fleming

159. *Janelle Monáe's The ArchAndroid* by Alyssa Favreau

160. *John Prine's John Prine* by Erin Osmon

161. *Maria Callas's Lyric and Coloratura Arias* by Ginger Dellenbaugh

162. *The National's Boxer* by Ryan Pinkard

163. *Kraftwerk's Computer World* by Steve Tupai Francis

164. *Cat Power's Moon Pix* by Donna Kozloskie

165. *George Michael's Faith* by Matthew Horton

166. *Kendrick Lamar's To Pimp a Butterfly* by Sequoia Maner

167. *Britney Spears's Blackout* by Natasha Lasky

168. *Earth, Wind & Fire's That's the Way of the World* by Dwight E. Brooks

169. *Minnie Riperton's Come to My Garden* by Brittnay L. Proctor

170. *Babes in Toyland's Fontanelle* by Selena Chambers

171. *Madvillain's Madvillainy* by Will Hagle

172. *ESG's Come Away with ESG* by Cheri Percy

173. *BBC Radiophonic Workshop's BBC Radiophonic Workshop: A Retrospective* by William Weir

174. *Living Colour's Time's Up* by Kimberly Mack

175. *The Go-Go's Beauty and the Beat* by Lisa Whittington-Hill

176. *Madonna's Erotica* by Michael Dango

177. *Body Count's Body Count* by Ben Apatoff